FAITH IN THE
AGE OF REASON

Faith in the Age of Reason

The Enlightenment from Galileo to Kant

Jonathan Hill

InterVarsity Press
Downers Grove, Illinois

La Pascaline – a
mechanical calculator
invented by Blaise Pascal
(1623–62). Musée des
Arts et Métiers, Paris.

Previous page:
A Philosopher Lecturing
on the Orrery (1764–66)
by Joseph Wright of
Derby (1734–97).

Page one: The earth and
moon, photographed
by the Galileo space
probe in 1992.

InterVarsity Press
P.O. Box 1400, Downers Grove, IL 60515-1426
World Wide Web: www.ivpress.com
E-mail: mail@ivpress.com

Copyright © 2004 Jonathan Hill

This edition copyright © 2004 Lion Hudson

Published in the United States of America by
InterVarsity Press, Downers Grove, Illinois,
with permission from Lion Hudson.

ISBN 0-8308-2360-3

Printed and bound in China

**Library of Congress Cataloging-in-Publication Data
has been requested**

P 15 14 13 12 11 10 9 8 7 6 5 4 3 2 1
Y 14 13 12 11 10 09 08 07 06 05 04

Contents

3|
7

115402

Introduction

Few can have summarized the Age of Reason as succinctly as Charles Dickens, in the famous opening words of *A Tale of Two Cities* of 1859:

It was the best of times, it was the worst of times, it was the age of wisdom, it was the age of foolishness, it was the epoch of belief, it was the epoch of incredulity, it was the season of Light, it was the season of Darkness, it was the spring of hope, it was the winter of despair, we had everything before us, we had nothing before us, we were all going direct to Heaven, we were all going direct the other way – in short, the period was so far like the present period, that some of its noisiest authorities insisted on its being received, for good or for evil, in the superlative degree of comparison only.

'The most formidable weapon against errors of every kind is Reason. I have never used any other, and I trust I never shall.'

THOMAS PAINE,
THE AGE OF REASON
PREFACE

It was, in many ways, a period unlike any other in history. For one thing, it was one of the few that named itself. No one in the Middle Ages thought of themselves as medieval, and the ancients were unaware that they were ancient; but the inhabitants of the Age of Reason, named after Tom Paine's book of 1793, knew exactly when they lived, and they were proud of it.

The term 'Age of Reason' is often used interchangeably with 'Enlightenment' – another word that the people of the time used themselves to describe it. The notion that the world had existed in varying stages of darkness beforehand, and that it was only at this point that everyone awoke from a kind of intellectual stupor, of course reflects both the optimism and the arrogance of the period itself. Yet it was during this time, more than any other, that our modern world was forged. Indeed, the modern period is generally thought to have begun some time in the seventeenth century. Many of the voices of that time sound remarkably familiar to us – we can identify with their concerns and their way of doing things. But it was also a time when older world views were still very powerful, and some of the great concerns of the age are as alien to us now as those of the ancient or medieval worlds that came before. It was in religion, above all, that this clash of world views took place. Our modern views of religion, like our modern understanding of science and the interaction between the two, were developed as the Enlightenment gathered pace and hit opposition.

This book looks at what these new ideas were that became so powerful during the Enlightenment, and what they did to Christianity. Unlike some of the other books in this series, the period presented here is a relatively short one – only a century and a half – and a rather vague one at that. I have chosen to begin the Age of Reason with the end of the Thirty Years War in 1648, and end it with the French Revolution in 1789 – essentially, the period when stockings and large wigs of one kind or another were considered the height of fashion for men, if not for women. But these are little more than convenient markers, and many of the people in the following pages worked at least partly outside these dates. As the first chapter suggests, the roots of the Enlightenment lie earlier than this, and as we see in the last chapter, we are still feeling its effects today. Indeed, there is a good case for saying that the Age of Reason has never ended, and we are still living in it now.

To set the Enlightenment in context, the first chapter describes what came before: the Middle Ages, the Renaissance and the Reformation, which bequeathed a whole set of assumptions and problems to the thinkers of the Age of Reason. The second chapter gives an overview of the Enlightenment, introducing the key figures and ideas of the time, together with the places and political context in which they lived.

The following chapters look in a little more detail at some of the broad themes of the Age of Reason. Chapter 3 focuses on the incredible scientific advances made during the period, while Chapter 4 describes the state of the churches and the ways in which they tried to deal with each other and with the new challenges of the age. And Chapter 5 looks at the new ideas of the philosophers, who

were forging the distinctively modern way of thinking of the world.

The new ideas of the Age of Reason represented a major threat to traditional religion, but at the same time they offered new opportunities as well, and this is the subject of the chapters that follow. Chapter 6 focuses on the problems of faith and authority that the new philosophy threw up, while Chapter 7 looks at how the new science and philosophy were causing problems with the traditional understanding of God and the world. Those problems led to deism and even atheism, the subject of Chapter 8.

Finally, Chapter 9 looks at how the Age of Reason came to an end, as political and intellectual revolutions forced a major revision of its assumptions – but how, in another way, we are still living in it ourselves.

Opposite page: The writer and philosopher Voltaire hosts a literary and scientific discussion. Like all good parties, this one seems to have spilled out onto the stairs.

CHAPTER 1

The Story So Far

The Enlightenment didn't simply appear from nowhere, as if someone turned on a light bulb one day. Like any other period in history, it grew out of what came before. And in some respects, it was a rebellion against earlier ideas and institutions, some of which had been held sacred for over a millennium.

The Middle Ages

The Middle Ages are normally thought to have lasted from around the sixth century to the fifteenth – everything from the end of the Roman empire in western Europe to the beginning of modern times. The first part of this period, known as the Dark Ages, was a time of great uncertainty: the empire, which had guaranteed political, cultural and religious uniformity throughout Europe, had collapsed. But in this political confusion, one new force for unity quickly arose – the Catholic Church and, in particular, the papacy. Among the competing nation states of Europe that developed, the one faith and the one church ensured a degree of cultural unity even greater, perhaps, than that of the old empire. While there was, of course, variation in what people believed, it is perhaps easier to talk of 'the medieval world view' than it is of 'the' ancient or modern one.

What did this world view involve? A detailed account can be found in G.R. Evans's *Faith in the Medieval World*, part of this series, but it was rooted in the notion of *authority*. In practical terms this meant the authority, above all, of the church; but the idea that the church was one source of authority, in competition with others such as scripture or science, would have been largely alien to the medieval mind. This idea of competing authorities would develop in the Reformation and the Enlightenment. The medieval world view, by contrast, was a wholly unified one. It was a conception of a complete body of knowledge – geographical, political, metaphysical, scientific and spiritual – whose different disciplines complemented each other perfectly. Different areas of knowledge might be known through different means, but these different means were not in competition. What the scientist learned studying the world would be corroborated by the theologian studying the Bible.

Naturally, this is something of a simplification, and this holistic understanding of authority and knowledge did not spring up overnight. Perhaps the most important figure in its development was Thomas Aquinas, a Dominican friar of the thirteenth century, and one of the supreme intellects of the Middle Ages. Aquinas believed that the ultimate source of truth was divine revelation, handed down in the teaching of the church and preserved in the Bible. The weightiest church authority – after scripture – was Augustine, the great fifth-century theologian. But truth could also be found in secular authorities, the most reliable being Aristotle, the Greek philosopher of the fourth century BC who by the end of the thirteenth century was regarded as *the* greatest non-theological authority. Aquinas and others like him, known as the 'scholastic' philosophers, sought to create a philosophy that was a seamless blend of Aristotelian logic and science and Augustinian theology, one where faith and reason corroborated each other effortlessly.

Like most ancient Greeks, Aristotle had believed that the earth was the centre of the universe, and that the sun, moon and planets revolved around it in circles. This was known as the Ptolemaic system, after the ancient astronomer, Ptolemy, who set it out most clearly; and it was universally accepted in the Middle Ages. Yet the system was not simply astronomical or geographical – it was also religious. It was thought that the fixed stars were placed on a sort of glass sphere that enclosed everything else, and that beyond this was heaven and God. Thus, the further

'Since faith rests upon infallible truth, and since the contrary of a truth can never be demonstrated, it is clear that the arguments brought against faith cannot be demonstrations, but are difficulties that can be answered.'

THOMAS AQUINAS, *SUMMA THEOLOGIAE* I.1.8

from the centre of the system you were, the closer you were to God, and the more perfect things were. Aristotle had argued that there is a fundamental difference between the regions below and above the moon – in the former, objects naturally move in a straight line towards the centre of the earth, while in the latter, they naturally move in circles around it. The circle is of course appropriate for the celestial regions, being the perfect shape, and Aristotle believed that, while there is change and decay below the moon, there is none above it, and it is this region that is most divine. Indeed, some philosophers believed that the planets and stars were made of some perfect substance, the famous 'fifth element', not found below the moon and which could not be corrupted. Hell was located at the centre of the earth, as far from God as possible.

Why is all this important? It shows perhaps the most fundamental element of the medieval world view. The world was defined by its relation to human beings, who were defined by their relation to God. The earth and its inhabitants were at the centre of the universe, but they were surrounded by God, and everything that happened did so within his divine providence. In the face of his awesome presence, the things that happened in this material life did not matter very much; what mattered was one's salvation, and that depended on how one stood with the visible element of the divine hierarchy, the Catholic Church.

'A good painter is to paint two things – men and the workings of men's minds.'

LEONARDO DA VINCI,
NOTEBOOKS

Yet barely had the medieval system reached its most perfect expression and development than the mighty edifice began to crumble. Throughout the fourteenth to the sixteenth centuries, new ways of thinking began to emerge and directly challenged the established order. Most of these movements come under the general heading of the 'Renaissance'.

The Renaissance

The Renaissance involved, essentially, the rejection of everything that the Middle Ages represented – in areas as diverse as philosophy, science, literature, geography, society, art and religion. At the same time, however, many people clung on to the old ways of looking at things. This meant that the Renaissance was not just a time of exciting exploration and discovery; it was a time of conflict and misunderstanding too.

Hercules and the Erymanthian Boar by Giambologna. The protagonist is naked and incredibly muscly to show the nobility of humanity.

The word 'Renaissance' means 'rebirth', a term that reflects the cyclical view of history that characterized it. Many of those involved in the Renaissance were inspired by the ancient world, and wanted to return to the ideals and culture of the ancient Greeks and Romans. They regarded the Middle Ages as a boring period of intellectual stupor during which those ideals had been lost, and they hoped to restore the world that had existed in the past.

Artists, therefore, revived ancient sculpture, and even made direct imitations of it. They depicted characters and events from pagan mythology instead of the Bible. Sculptors such as Michelangelo celebrated the power and beauty of the human form, on the model of ancient Greek statues. In addition to the old ideal of aiding the pious worship of God, many artists now championed a defiant exultation of humanity. It was a bold, new departure.

Meanwhile, others were rebelling against the traditional authorities which had held sway in the universities for so long. One element of this was the conscious revival of pagan Neoplatonism, in opposition to the Christianized Aristotle. Another, more radical, was the development of what we can recognize as modern science.

One of the key figures in this was Francis Bacon, who was not only a philosopher but a statesman and courtier. While never really in favour with Queen Elizabeth, he did rise to become Lord Chancellor under James I – before being stripped of his title after two years for taking bribes, and living out his days in some disgrace. He is supposed to have died in 1626 after catching a cold from stuffing a chicken with snow to see if it would preserve it. It was a fitting way to go, because Bacon's philosophy revolved around the

Neoplatonism

What do you do if the intellectual world is dominated by the authority of one ancient Greek philosopher, and you're sick of him? Simple – you try to replace him with another ancient Greek philosopher.

That might seem to us a strange thing to do, but it made perfect sense in Renaissance times. Plato had been the teacher of Aristotle, and had been an enormous influence on western thought. He and his followers believed in a higher, intellectual, spiritual world, of which the physical world is simply a pale reflection. In later antiquity, this developed into 'Neoplatonism', which emphasized the mystical aspects of the system. Neoplatonism was a very important influence on early Christian theologians, especially Augustine; and through him it remained central to medieval Christianity. This was rather odd, given that Plato was traditionally regarded as the great rival to Aristotle, who was meant to be the supreme intellectual authority in the Middle Ages.

What happened in the Renaissance is that some philosophers, eager to break with the thought of the Middle Ages and the authority of Aristotle, came out in support of his rival, Plato. They tried to uncover what they regarded as the original, true philosophy, which had become obscured and covered over with the weaker thought of Aristotle. The greatest of these thinkers was Marsilio Ficino, who although a Catholic priest, sought to create a new philosophical and religious synthesis, based on Neoplatonic philosophy. Ficino regarded the human soul as the centre of the universe, containing within it all things. Contemplation of spiritual reality through the soul leads ultimately to union with God. This highly mystical approach to the universe went along with a lack of interest in traditional doctrine, and Ficino believed that all the world's religions offered different routes to God, reflecting his different facets. By the time he died in 1499, Ficino had not only put Neoplatonism back at the top of the agenda; he had provided a powerful philosophical and mystical underpinning of the Renaissance faith in human nature and human powers.

importance of experiment. He rejected the medieval synthesis of reason and revelation, arguing instead that some things are known through revelation, and everything else by experiment. He believed that if you carefully observe enough phenomena, the underlying natural laws will become obvious.

Despite the importance of his methodological theories, Bacon himself was not much of a scientist, but other Renaissance figures were busy putting the principles of experiment into action. William Harvey – Bacon's medical attendant – discovered the circulation of the blood. Johannes Kepler revolutionized astronomy – and launched a frontal assault on Aristotle's theories – by showing that the planets move in ellipses, not circles as everyone had assumed before. And, most of all, Galileo swept aside the laws of physics that Aristotle had laid down. He may not really have dropped weights off the Leaning Tower of Pisa during the course of his research, but he did carry out many similar experiments to demonstrate how the laws of motion and inertia really work.

Perhaps the most representative figure of the Renaissance, with all its contradictions, was a strange character who rejoiced in the name Philippus Aureolus Theophrastus Bombastus von Hohenheim. He, however, preferred to call himself 'Paracelsus', adding the title, 'Philosopher of the Monarchia, Prince of Spagyrists, Chief Astronomer, Surpassing Physician and Trismegistus of Mechanical Arcana', which gives some idea of the range not only of his interests but also of his ego. This prickly, arrogant, brilliant physician spent most of his life outraging the authorities and moving (or being forcibly transferred) from university to university throughout Europe. The natural sciences at this time, including medicine, were rather like theology: there were accepted authorities on the subject, whose books one studied and whose theories one expounded. Indeed, some scholarly physicians spent all their time doing this, and never met a patient.

'I have taken all knowledge to be my province.'

FRANCIS BACON,
LETTER TO LORD
BURLEIGH, 1592

Paracelsus
(Philippus
Aureolus
Theophrastus
Bombast von
Hohenheim),
physician and
philosopher.
Contemporary
copy of a lost
portrait by
Quentin Massys
(1466–1530).

FAMOSO·DOCTOR   PARESELSVS

Paracelsus, however, had no time for traditional authorities. He was a contemporary of Luther, and his place in science has been compared to that of the great Reformer in religion. He went so far as to burn the works of Galen and other medieval authorities in public. He argued that diseases are actually caused by external agents, and they can be cured by the application of substances derived from the natural world. The cures he effected by this method were astonishing to his contemporaries, and he was regarded as a miracle-worker and a magician.

In fact, Paracelsus really was a magician. At one level his theories sound very modern to us, and so does his scientific method: instead of perusing ancient books in dusty libraries, he believed, like Bacon, that knowledge comes from going out into the world and studying nature at first hand. But he did so in a mystical way: he believed that the reason we can understand the world is that the whole universe is reflected within the human soul, and that true knowledge comes about through introspection. He shared, too, the fascination of his age with the notion of occult and esoteric secrets; his works are full of strange code-words and deliberately opaque jargon, and he loves to hint at mysteries and secrets of which he is forbidden to speak. Indeed, some elements of Paracelsus's science have essentially been lost, because no one can understand what he is on about.

This mystical, esoteric approach is reflected too in Paracelsus's understanding of the natural world. He believed that natural objects are divided into two classes – helpful and harmful – and that providence has scattered clues throughout nature to help us tell which is which. For example, a prickly plant might contain a chemical that helps to cure scratches. This is the famous 'doctrine of signatures'. Paracelsus was the first to believe that chemicals extracted from plants might be useful in medicine, and his research in this field makes him the true founder of modern chemistry; but he regarded his work as alchemy, and claimed not only to have manufactured the mythical 'fifth element' but also to have created gold from base substances (although he didn't regard this as any great achievement!). As a magician, alchemist and spiritualist, Paracelsus was very much a man of his time.

The condemnation of Galileo

The Renaissance was a confusing time, as new ideas interacted with the old, and many people were not at all happy with the proposed overthrow of the medieval authorities – which is why Paracelsus could never hold down

'The Monarchy of all the Arts has been at length derived and conferred on me, Theophrastus Paracelsus, Prince of Philosophy and of Medicine. For this purpose I have been chosen by God to extinguish and blot out all the phantasies of elaborate and false works, of delusive and presumptuous words.'

PARACELSUS,
*THE TINCTURE OF
THE PHILOSOPHERS*
PREFACE

a job. By far the most famous outcome of this was the condemnation of Galileo, who was found guilty by the Inquisition in 1633 of teaching that the earth moves, and forbidden from repeating the heresy. This is usually thought of as a case of science clashing with religion – the Catholic Church overreacting to a perceived challenge to its authority, and trying to silence the voice of reason and progress – but in fact the situation was a little more complex.

**Engraving of
Copernican Solar
System, 1661.**

When the astronomer Copernicus proposed in the early sixteenth century that the earth goes round the sun, he didn't really have any good evidence to support his claim. His ideas remained controversial, and only a minority of scientists accepted them. One of those who did was Johannes Kepler, a German mathematician and astronomer, who died in 1630. His observations of the planets and their satellites did much to support

Copernicus's ideas, and together with those of his contemporary and correspondent Galileo, they provided a powerful case for the new understanding of how the universe worked. Unfortunately, it was a theory that completely contradicted all traditional science, not to mention the authority of Aristotle. As we have seen, the Ptolemaic system was not simply a theory about how the universe is constructed; it was an image of fundamental importance, showing how the universe works. To challenge the Ptolemaic system was to challenge the whole medieval way of thinking.

Galileo's dispute was therefore not just with the Catholic Church: indeed, the early Reformers, including Martin Luther, rejected the Copernican theory as well. More fundamentally, Galileo was trying to overthrow Aristotle and the whole philosophical and scientific orthodoxy that had held sway for centuries. It was, essentially, a clash of the old, authoritative understanding of philosophy, with the new, experimental way of doing science. Galileo lost, but his method – not just his Copernicanism – would win out in the end. In the meantime, however, there was a lot of disagreement, as the old and the new ways of thinking coexisted.

'This fool wishes to reverse the entire science of astronomy; but sacred scripture tells us that Joshua commanded the sun to stand still, and not the earth.'

MARTIN LUTHER,
TABLE TALK

Martin Luther

If Galileo was a victim of the clash between old and new, that was nothing to what had happened a century earlier to Martin Luther – a figure so significant that it has been estimated that more books have been written about him than about anyone else in history, other than Jesus himself. Luther was an enormously charismatic monk and academic who rebelled against what he saw as the corruptions of the Catholic Church, and who, in so doing, helped inspire a massive wave of protest and change – the Reformation.

Opposite page:
Luther, still dressed as an Augustinian monk, faces the judgment of the Emperor Charles V at the Diet of Worms in 1521. Painting, 1872, by Paul Thumann (1834–1908).

The Reformation grew, in part, out of the humanistic ideals of the Renaissance. Luther's protest was partly inspired by a desire to get back to original, authentic Christianity – just as the thinkers of the Renaissance hoped to sweep aside the obfuscations of the Middle Ages and return to the purity of the ancient world. He believed that authentic Christianity could be found most clearly in Paul's letter to the Romans, which teaches that the believer is saved by faith alone, and not by works. Luther took this to mean that all the paraphernalia of medieval Christendom served only to obscure the essence of Christianity: it deluded people into thinking that they could buy salvation, or earn it, or be given it by priests.

'In my heart reigns this one article, faith in my dear Lord Christ, the beginning, middle and end of whatever spiritual and divine thoughts I may have, whether by day or by night.'

MARTIN LUTHER,
*COMMENTARY
ON GALATIANS*
INTRODUCTION

By the time Luther died in 1546, the church had been split. Throughout Europe, people had formed new churches, rebelling against the power of priests. They had thrown off what they regarded as the corruptions of the Middle Ages: the pomp and ceremony of the liturgy, the 'magical' manipulation of the elements at the Mass, the special status of the priests.

The later Reformation

Luther was both a catalyst and symptom of a major tide of reform which swept through the church in the sixteenth century. While whole congregations split away from the

power of Rome to form the new Protestant churches, there were many voices successfully calling for reform within the Catholic Church itself. The Council of Trent was called in 1545, partly in response to the criticisms of Luther and those like him. While the Council rejected the new theology of Protestantism, including its shibboleths of 'salvation by faith alone' and 'the authority of scripture alone', it did tacitly recognize that the Reformers had had a point in their criticisms of clerical abuses and corruption throughout the church. Major steps were therefore taken to curb abuses, improve the education of priests, and generally put Rome's house in order.

If Luther was the outstanding figure of the first generation of Reformers, his natural successor in the second generation was John Calvin. Calvin spent most of his life in Geneva, which he transformed into a kind of Protestant theocracy: under his guidance, the city became the leading centre of Protestant thought, the 'Protestant Rome'. Calvin himself forged a new understanding of the Protestant faith, in his sermons and biblical commentaries, and most of all in his famous *Institutes of the Christian Religion*, in which he sought to present the Christian faith in a systematic way, based upon the teaching of the Bible.

Calvin's life and teachings laid the basis for what became known as the 'Reformed' Church, although 'Calvinism' – the movement inspired by his theology – spread beyond it into other Christian traditions too. In fact, the Reformed Church enjoyed considerably more success than the Lutheran. Where Lutheranism was largely confined to the German-speaking parts of Europe, and Scandinavia, the Reformed Church spread throughout the continent, not only to France but also to Scotland and, above all, the Netherlands. As we shall see in Chapter 4, the theological temperature rose steadily over the following century, as theologians from the different churches not only attacked each other, but were also riven by internal dissensions.

Worst of all, the tension spilled out of the pulpit and the lecture hall onto the battlefield. In 1572, in the course of civil war in France as different factions struggled for the crown, Catholic troops killed 20,000 Protestant civilians in Paris and throughout France. The St Bartholomew Massacre, as the atrocity was known, did not exactly ease relations between the Catholic and Reformed

'To sum up in a word: if the eyes of believers are turned towards the power of the resurrection, then, in their hearts, the cross of Christ will at last triumph over the devil, flesh, sin, and the wicked.'

JOHN CALVIN,
*INSTITUTES OF THE
CHRISTIAN RELIGION*
III.IX.6

churches, and the tension would break out even more catastrophically in the Thirty Years War. This was really a series of conflicts between a variety of different European powers, that occurred for a variety of reasons throughout the first half of the seventeenth century. It began in 1618, when the Protestant Bohemians rose up in revolt against the Catholic Hapsburgs, the rulers of Austria. The Spanish and Catholic German states came to the support of their Catholic friends in Austria, while the French, English and Dutch allied with the German and Bohemian Protestants. In other words, political and national grievances pulled the various powers of Europe into a series of military alliances that formed along largely religious lines. And religious differences were an important motivation in the war: Ferdinand II, for example, the Hapsburg emperor, was a devout and sincere Catholic who believed it was his mission to call upon the forces of the church to root out the pernicious heresy of Protestantism. This was the first great pan-European war, prefiguring the even worse horrors of the First and Second World Wars three centuries later. It is estimated that, between 1618 and 1648, the population of the Hapsburg empire, riven not only by the fighting but by the disease and starvation that came in its wake, dropped from 21 million to 13.5 million.

The Age of Reason

The Thirty Years War ended in 1648 with the Peace of Westphalia. But decades of bitter fighting had left a ravaged continent, and a people sick of conflict, both military and theological. The decades after 1648 were by no means a peaceful time to live in Europe: on the contrary, they saw, among other things, the English Civil War and the execution of King Charles I, and more wars between the European powers, although all were on a smaller scale. There were also, naturally, the usual revolutions, great fires, and so on. However, even as the Thirty Years War was dragging to a much-desired end, there was a new spirit brewing in Europe: one that was desperate to make a clean break with the past, and the religious tension, arid scholasticism, petty bickering and occult fetishism that the Renaissance and Reformation seemed to have produced. By 1648, the seeds of the Enlightenment, which would hold sway over Europe for the next century and a half, had been well and truly sown.

A new Europe

The new breed of thinkers inhabited a very different continent from their forebears. Sixteenth-century Europe had been dominated by the staunchly Catholic power of Spain, a country that, in 1492, had achieved the twin coup of eliminating the lingering Muslim presence from its territory and discovering America. Spain shared its dominance with Italy, the cradle of the Renaissance, and a region which, although it had no real political power, exercised an awesome cultural sway over the continent.

Fifty years later, everything had changed. Spain, exhausted by the Thirty Years War, had had its wings clipped: hegemony had passed from the west and south of Europe to its centre. France, bordered by has-been Spain on one side and the devastated states of Germany on the other, arose as the new superpower of the continent. The Netherlands, which had previously been under Spanish rule, won their freedom with the Treaty of Westphalia in 1648, and almost overnight became the world's leading trading nation. Amsterdam was the exchange capital of the world, and the Dutch merchant fleet was the largest on the planet.

Europe was also now freed, to a considerable extent, from the external dangers which had previously threatened it. Until the fifteenth century, the might of the Islamic nations had been lapping at the borders of the continent, culminating in the fall of Constantinople to the Ottomans in 1453. But in 1492 the last Muslim strongholds in Spain were taken, and the seventeenth century saw the confirmation of a terminal decline on the part of the Muslim powers, at least from the European point of view. In 1683, despite being outnumbered five to one, the Polish king John Sobieski successfully routed the Ottoman forces besieging Vienna. The days when Turkey threatened to bring Europe to its knees were over, and it was well on the way to becoming the 'sick man of Europe' that so exercised the concerns of nineteenth-century politicians.

The new Europe, then, was a Europe of independent nations: of trade and colonialism, of a rising middle class. Instead of the old hegemonies of the past, when a single power, whether emperor or pope, sought to govern the continent, a new ideal arose of a 'balance of power' between different states – and between the churches too. The controlling hand of the pope had been declawed, even in Catholic countries, by the Treaty of Westphalia, which permitted every state to follow whatever religion it saw fit. Although France, the new dominant force in central

Europe, was largely Catholic, it was a slightly idiosyncratic sort of Catholicism that tended not to listen very carefully to anything coming from Rome. And the Netherlands, of course, were fiercely Calvinist. It was a world in which notions such as nationhood, human rights and law were inevitably going to play an increasingly important role, and they were going to be rethought along rationalist, not religious, lines.

A new world view

As its name might suggest, the most cherished ideal of the Age of Reason was reason itself: the human capacity, by means of investigation rather than by relying on external authority, to *understand*. In the first half of the seventeenth century, two philosophers, the Englishman Thomas Hobbes and the Frenchman René Descartes, pioneered a new way of understanding the world and the mind. Instead of the Neoplatonic world of the Renaissance, dominated by occult forces, where objects exerted mysterious 'influences' on each other, they sought to understand the world in mechanistic terms. For them, the universe is essentially a clanking contraption of levers, pulleys and ball bearings – albeit an extremely complicated one. Nevertheless, its mechanistic nature means that it is perfectly comprehensible to anyone who takes the time to study it.

At the same time, there was a desire to forget the old divisions of the past and embrace what was common to all humanity. One important movement of the time, which we shall see in more detail in Chapter 4, was that of 'syncretism', which sought to reunite the different churches of Europe. A leading figure in this was the Dutch Reformed thinker Hugo Grotius, who felt that Christians of all denominations should come together on the basis of their common faith and heritage. For this, Grotius was arrested by the less liberally minded Calvinists who at that time ran the Netherlands, and spent some years in prison until he made a daring escape and fled the country.

Despite his work as a theologian, however, Grotius is

'God has given conscience a judicial power to be the sovereign guide of human actions, by despising whose admonitions the mind is stupefied into brutal hardness.'

HUGO GROTIUS,
ON THE LAW OF PEACE AND WAR
BOOK II, CHAPTER 23

most remembered as a legal theorist. His *On the Law of Peace and War* of 1625 was the first major study of the theory of international law, and in it he sought to place binding human laws – transcending national boundaries – on a naturalistic and rational footing. This kind of thinking was partly the result of the application to philosophy and theology of the laissez-faire principles which nations such as the Netherlands were applying to economics with such remarkable success.

Free trade and tolerance: the Dutch Enlightenment

It took 80 years of intermittent warfare, but the Netherlands finally achieved their independence from Spain in 1648. The country had already become a great trading nation, and during the seventeenth century entered something of a golden age, quickly becoming established as one of the most powerful nations in Europe. Culture, the arts and science all flourished, with the works of the seventeenth-century Dutch painters quickly becoming established as classics to rank alongside the best that the Italian Renaissance had produced.

A view of the
Regulierspoort,
Amsterdam,
in winter,
by Abraham
Beerstraten,
(1622–66).
Johnny van
Haeften Gallery.
London.

The Netherlands were the foremost bastion of the Reformed faith in Europe. It was to here that Calvinists suffering persecution elsewhere, such as in Catholic France under Louis XIV, or in England under the Anglo-Catholic Charles I, emigrated. It was here, above all, that Reformed theologians set about defining and refining their faith, a process that led to the explosive Arminian controversy, which we shall see in Chapter 4. Indeed, those who deviated from the party line here – known as

'Remonstrants' – could find that the orthodox Calvinists,
or 'Non-Remonstrants', were capable of being just
as inflexible as any Catholic had been during the
Reformation. Grotius had been lucky to suffer only
imprisonment for his Remonstrant views – others were
executed.

Nevertheless, these persecutions paled into
insignificance beside what the French and English
authorities were capable of, and the effective rule of
merchants meant that the Netherlands were renowned,
above all, for tolerance – racial, philosophical and national.
It was to the Netherlands that substantial Jewish
communities, fleeing the persecutions of Philip II in Spain
in the sixteenth century, had come. Charles II of England
had sought refuge here after his father's execution, as had
John Locke's patron, the disgraced Lord Shaftesbury. It
was here, too, that philosophers and religious thinkers
considered heterodox by their contemporaries, such as
Descartes and his notorious disciple Spinoza, found
sanctuary and worked. In providing an environment in

which their ideas could develop, free of interference, the
wealthy mercantile ruling classes of the Netherlands
played a key role in the evolution of the Enlightenment in
the seventeenth century, and in the development of one of
its key doctrines – tolerance.

Enlightenment and liberalism: an axis of reason

If one person could have claimed to be the most powerful
man in the world in the late seventeenth century, it would
have to have been Louis XIV of France. The 'Sun King' of
legend ascended to the throne in 1643, at the age of four,
and remained there until his death in 1715. When Cardinal
Mazarin – effectively the prime minister – died in 1661, the
23-year-old king decided not to appoint a successor to run
the country for him, and instead did it himself. Whether or
not he really uttered the famous words, 'The state – that's
me,' under his personal rule France was established as the
leading force for culture and enlightenment in the world.
The magnificent palace of Versailles – completed in 1682
after 20 years of construction – with its legendary gardens

Just a small
corner of the
gardens of
Versailles.

symbolized the spirit of the age. It was an age of formalism, geometry, beauty and intellect. And where France led, Europe followed. Fifty years earlier, scholars had communicated in Latin. Some still did, but French had now largely replaced the medieval tongue as the international language of culture.

At the same time, Louis did everything he could to extend France's political power, which he achieved by means of a remarkably aggressive foreign policy. The

Bossuet and the Catholic Enlightenment

Born in 1627, Jacques Bossuet was a man of refinement, learning and devout piety. He was educated by the Jesuits and won considerable renown as an eloquent preacher. Louis XIV made him tutor to his son, for whom the enthusiastic Bossuet wrote a number of textbooks on a range of subjects. Bossuet was clearly a man with considerable clout in French intellectual circles, and in 1682 it was he who drew up the 'Gallican Articles', the classical statement of Gallicanism, after an assembly of the French clergy. Bossuet believed in the infallibility of the Catholic Church, but it was an infallibility that derived from its apostolic foundation and tradition, rather than one that resided in the person of the pope. The falsity of Protestantism was, in his eyes, guaranteed simply by its novelty, which meant that it had abandoned the fundamental apostolic principle. Nevertheless, Bossuet engaged sympathetically with non-Catholics, especially Anglicans, writing books about Catholicism intended for a Protestant readership, and engaging in rational debates with leading Protestants. His high-minded, persuasive, intellectual faith was typical of men of his ilk and nationality. It exemplifies the form that the mainstream of the Enlightenment took in the seventeenth century – enlightened, reasonable Christianity – which would give way, in the eighteenth century, to an enlightened, reasonable hostility to established religion.

'Men are all born subjects: and the paternal empire, which accustoms them to obey, accustoms them at the same time to have only one leader.'

JACQUES BOSSUET,
POLITICS DRAWN FROM HOLY SCRIPTURE BOOK II, PROP. 7

wealth of the Netherlands, so close to hand, tempted him into a series of wars with the Dutch, and in 1689 he plunged the world into a conflict that threatened devastation of a kind not seen for 50 years – the War of the Grand Alliance, during which the fighting covered Europe, Ireland and North America. Barely had that finished, in 1697, before Louis launched the War of the Spanish Succession of 1701–14, which left his grandson occupying the throne of Spain.

Jacques Bossuet, possibly wondering why all the curtains are falling down. Portrait by Hyacinthe Rigaud (1649–1743).

The age over which Louis presided was an avowedly Catholic one. His famous slogan was '*Une foi, une loi, une roi*' – 'One faith, one law, one king', and as that suggests, it was a nationalistic sort of Catholicism rather than a papal one. In sharp contrast to the Catholicism of Philip II, who had always been keen to demonstrate his loyalty to the pope, the Catholicism of Louis XIV and of France was a religion that would be defended to the last by its adherents because it was the ancestral faith of their country, not because of deference to an Italian potentate. This kind of attitude is known as 'Gallicanism', and one of its leading proponents in the court of the Sun King was Jacques Bossuet, the famous Catholic bishop of Meaux.

Despite the benign influence of men such as Bossuet, however, the king's determination to unite his subjects under a single faith inevitably took less admirable forms. Of the 15 million or so inhabitants of France – the largest population of any European state – about 1 million were Calvinists, known as Huguenots. Their freedom to worship

The Catholic authorities try to force a French Protestant to renounce his faith. *The Huguenot*, undated engraving.

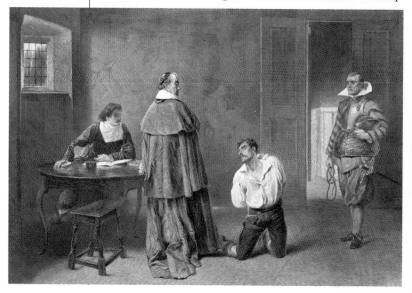

was guaranteed by the Edict of Nantes of 1598, but Louis saw to it that things were not easy for them: they suffered restrictions on where they could go, what professions they could take up, where they could worship, what schools they could attend. In 1681, the oppression became suppression, as the army was ordered to harrass Huguenots until they converted. Four years later, the inevitable happened, and the king revoked the Edict of Nantes.

Little wonder, then, that a growing number of French intellectuals were beginning to think that religion didn't seem to offer much of a basis for an enlightened modern society. It wouldn't be long before some were questioning the point of religion at all. In the meantime, many were enormously impressed by a neighbouring country that seemed to be working out a far more satisfactory social philosophy, a philosophy of reason and liberalism.

England was, on the surface, having a harder time of it than France. Politically, most of the seventeenth century was something of a disaster, involving as it did a civil war, the establishment of a short-lived republic, and the overthrow of two monarchs – a chain of events that led to the 'Glorious Revolution' of 1688 and the coronation of the Dutch William of Orange as King of England – a man who was invited to invade the country by a parliament desperate to secure a Protestant monarch.

As England was finally establishing some political stability, it was fostering major intellectual developments that would put the country on a cultural par with France. Unsurprisingly, given their immediate history, the British thinkers of the time were pioneering new ideas about government, politics, ethics and economics, ideas that aimed to avoid the extremes that absolutist monarchs such as Charles I or despots such as Oliver Cromwell had slipped into. Where continental states were developing an ever-higher reverence for their monarchies, the bloody political and military struggles of seventeenth-century England had essentially been a process of the gradual erosion of the rights of the monarch. During this time,

'We forbid our subjects of the so-called Reformed religion to meet any more for the exercise of the said religion... We enjoin all ministers of the said religion... to leave our kingdom and the territories subject to us within a fortnight of the publication of our present edict.'

THE REVOCATION
OF THE EDICT OF
NANTES, 1685

'I tell you we will cut off his head with the crown upon it.'

OLIVER CROMWELL,
DURING CHARLES I'S
TRIAL

*'It is an easy
thing, for men to
be deceived, by
the specious
name of
Libertie.'*

THOMAS HOBBES,
LEVIATHAN II,
CHAPTER 21

the idea had taken hold that the king rules only by the permission of the people, who retain the ability to judge or even remove him if they don't approve of his policies or his religion. King Charles I, with his dogged insistence upon his own divine vocation, had underestimated the strength that this conviction had for some of his most powerful subjects. That made his encounter with the executioner's axe in 1649 inevitable. He had no place in a world where an English parliament could, in effect, vote out one king and vote in another, as happened in 1688; a world in which concepts such as liberty, the rights of the individual and liberalism were being forged.

The process was kick-started by Hobbes, who sought to create a new political theory that, like his account of the physical world, was rational and humanist, without any reliance on religion or the occult. In his famous *Leviathan* of 1651, Hobbes put forward the radical claim that government is based upon natural law, not upon

The Father of the Enlightenment

John Locke was born in Somerset in 1632, the son of a Puritan clerk. His family just had the means to send him to Oxford, where he became a medical doctor. He later became attached to Lord Shaftesbury, a major figure at the court of Charles II. Indeed, Shaftesbury owed his life to Locke, who in 1668 oversaw an operation on his patron's liver – a highly risky procedure at the time, the success of which was testament to Locke's skill. Throughout this period, Locke travelled all around Europe, as his patron's political fortunes sometimes necessitated beating a hasty retreat from London; indeed, in 1683, his circle was implicated in a plot against the king, and Shaftesbury fled to the Netherlands, where he died.

Locke returned to England and a public life in 1688, with the 'Glorious Revolution' of William of Orange, and acted as an intellectual adviser to the court, while also working at the Board of Trade. He spent most of his time writing, however, on philosophical and religious topics. His *Essay Concerning Human Understanding*, published in 1690, together with *The Reasonableness of Christianity* of 1695, established him as a household name. He died in 1704.

divine sanction, and that a government exists only by the will of the people.

However, the appearance of modern 'liberalism' was associated above all with John Locke, one of the most prominent British intellectuals at the turn of the eighteenth century. Locke is perhaps most famous for his political ideas, and his values of tolerance and liberalism, which would have an enormous impact in both America and France. Like Hobbes before him, Locke was keen to develop a new understanding of how society and its members operate and interact. He was inspired in this by the incredible advances that had been made by science over the preceding century – culminating in the work of Isaac Newton, a man revered throughout England as a living genius, a new Aristotle. If the exercise of cool mathematical reason could produce Newton's *Principia*, regarded by many as the final word in the study of physics, who could say what it might produce in other spheres as well?

Frontispiece and title page with a portrait of John Locke from *The Works of John Locke*, vol 1, 4th edition. London 1740.

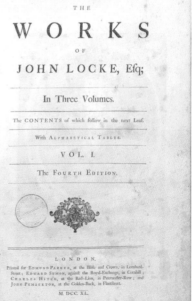

THE

WORKS

OF

JOHN LOCKE, Esq;

In Three Volumes.

The CONTENTS of which follow in the next Leaf.

With ALPHABETICAL TABLES.

VOL. I.

The FOURTH EDITION.

LONDON,

Printed for EDMUND PARKER, at the Bible and Crown, in Lombard-Street; EDWARD SYMON, against the Royal-Exchange, in Cornhill; CHARLES HITCH, at the Red-Lion, in Paternoster-Row; and JOHN PEMBERTON, at the Golden-Buck, in Fleetstreet.

M. DCC. XL.

Locke's attempts to do this in philosophy, psychology, politics and religion resulted in his starting the English Enlightenment virtually single-handedly. Locke believed that human reason should be the final arbiter of what we believe, in politics, ethics and religion alike; and he believed that the values of tolerance and individual liberty, of education and freedom, would provide the proper environment for the edifying exercise of reason. This philosophy was the philosophy of the Enlightenment in a nutshell. Yet despite his enormous prestige at home, Locke's influence was greatest on continental Europe. French intellectuals, many of whom spent much of their time ingratiating themselves with the glorious court of the Sun King, were enormously impressed by the common-sense political philosophy coming from across the Channel. Between them, Britain and France were responsible for the most characteristic trends and movements of the Enlightenment.

Crushing infamy: Voltaire and the French philosophers
If a single individual could be identified as the central figure of the Enlightenment, epitomizing its values and dreams, its horizons and its limits, that man would be François Marie Arouet – known to the world by his pen name, Voltaire. He was the dominant cultural force of his day, and the smiling figure he presents in contemporary paintings, with a wicked glint in his eye, conveys the intellectual power, wit and irreverence that characterized his version of the Enlightenment.

Born in 1694 in Paris, Voltaire was educated by the Jesuits and quickly became known for his satirical poetry and biting wit. His penchant for attacking the aristocracy in his work earned him 11 months in the Bastille, and it forced him into exile in 1726. He spent three years in England imbibing the values of liberalism, rationalism and religious tolerance. Upon his return to France in 1729, Voltaire set out to enlighten France by extolling the virtues of the British philosophers, above all Locke and Newton.

In his *Philosophical Letters* of 1734, which he called 'the first bomb against the Old Regime', he compared France's government, science and philosophy unfavourably to England's. This led to his expulsion once again from Paris. Voltaire headed for the French countryside, where he immersed himself in the study of the natural sciences. In 1749, at the invitation of Frederick the Great, he moved to Prussia for a few years. He eventually ended up in Switzerland, where he devoted himself to writing plays, essays, novels and articles. His success was so great, and his influence so enormous, that his estate became a place of pilgrimage to writers, philosophers and people of culture of every kind – to such an extent that he was known as 'the innkeeper of Europe'. In 1778, in order to direct one of his own plays, Voltaire returned to Paris to enormous acclaim, but died in the city shortly afterwards.

'Liberty of thought is the life of the soul.'

VOLTAIRE, *ESSAY ON EPIC POETRY*

Voltaire devoted his life and work to the principles of reason and tolerance that he saw exemplified in British philosophy. His slogan was 'Crush infamy!' and to Voltaire the most infamous institution in France was the Roman Catholic Church, an organization which in his eyes demanded loyalty from its members, which forced upon them a ridiculous and barbarous mythology, and which put down dissenters with the sword. Voltaire was not an irreligious man, and was one of the foremost proponents of 'deism' – a movement which, as we shall see in Chapter 8, sought to honour God without the historical trappings and superstition of traditional religion. Yet he was notorious as the arch-heretic and enemy of Christianity for the contempt with which he held what he regarded as the superstitious and authoritarian elements of the religion. Voltaire attacked the doctrines and practices of Christianity as mercilessly as he lampooned the secular rulers of society. There is a story that his local bishop once ordered that under no circumstances was Voltaire to be admitted to Mass. Voltaire, who had no intention of letting a mere bishop exercise authority over him, therefore faked a terminal

'Republics end with luxury; monarchies with poverty.'

BARON
MONTESQUIEU, *THE SPIRIT OF THE LAWS*
BOOK VII, CHAPTER 4

illness and forced a priest to give him the sacrament, which could not be denied to a man on his deathbed. The moment he had consumed it, Voltaire jumped out of bed and went for a walk. The notion that one could eat God was as blasphemous to him as it was ludicrous, and mockery was the only appropriate response to it.

At the time of his death, Voltaire had produced around 2,000 books and pamphlets. Perhaps the greatest was his *Philosophical Dictionary* of 1764, devoted primarily to ethical and religious subjects. The fact that this work was burnt throughout France showed that few in authority had heeded his *Treatise on Tolerance* of the previous year, in which Voltaire had condemned the atrocities that had been perpetrated throughout history in the name of religion and called for the freedom of each individual to practise whatever religion they chose.

Yet Voltaire was no iconoclast, a lone voice in the wilderness. On the contrary, while his voice may have been the loudest and most notorious, it was accompanied by a whole chorus of French critics, writers and philosophers, all of whom extolled reason and human progress and were critical to varying degrees of the traditional authorities and mores. The first and most famous of these *philosophes*, as they were known, was Baron Montesquieu. His *Persian Letters*, published in 1721, took the form of a series of letters by two fictitious Persians travelling throughout Europe, and in them Montesquieu bitterly satirized the establishment of his day: the French king, the French government, French society and, above all, the Catholic Church, which Montesquieu hated for much the same reasons as Voltaire. However, Montesquieu's attitude to Christianity softened over the years, and he was much more sympathetic to it in his most famous work, *The Spirit of the Laws* of 1748, which attempted to set out legal principles and the best ways to ensure that they worked.

One *philosophe* who never moderated his views was Baron d'Holbach, another aristocratic Frenchman (albeit of German birth), whose estate was often used as a meeting place by the others. D'Holbach was not only an atheist – a much more daring position than the deism of Voltaire – but believed that atheism was the only possible basis for a reasonable ethical system. Politically, he opposed all kinds of absolutism, including even the enlightened monarchies of the sort that Louis XIV had tried to create. Here again we see the strong influence of British thought. In his *System of Nature* of 1770, d'Holbach set forth a wholly materialistic and mechanistic understanding of the world. It is hard to imagine a more different figure from Bossuet a century earlier: such was the radical turnaround, from supporting religion to undermining it, that the French Enlightenment had taken.

'Many immoral men have attacked religion because it went against their inclinations. Many wise men have despised it because they thought it was ridiculous... But it is as a citizen that I attack it, because it seems to me that it is harmful to the wellbeing of the state, hostile to the march of the mind of man, and opposed to sound morality.'

BARON D'HOLBACH,
*CHRISTIANITY
UNVEILED*

The German Enlightenment

Compared to England, France and the Netherlands,
Germany took a long time to join the Enlightenment. This
was partly due to the state of the country after the Thirty
Years War, which was one of devastation and exhaustion:
it has been estimated that the population shrank from
20 million before the war to just 7 million after it. There
was also the fact that Germany was not a country at all but
a large collection of small independent statelets, united by
the German language, but divided between Catholic and
Lutheran churches.

The relatively low regard for modern culture in
Germany at this time is illustrated by the fact that
Newton, Locke and Voltaire were lionized in their own
countries, but their equivalent in Germany, Gottfried
Wilhelm von Leibniz, was never an especially popular
figure at home, at least in his lifetime. Yet he was,
perhaps, one of the most brilliant men not only of his day,
but of all time. He was born in 1646 in Leipzig, the son of
a professor of moral philosophy, and studied law before
taking up with a disreputable group of alchemists, and
working for the Elector of Mainz.

Leibniz came to the attention of the cultural world in
1672, when he was sent on a semi-ambassadorial mission
to Paris. The ostensible purpose of this was to present
Louis XIV with a plan he had worked out for the invasion
of Egypt, by which he hoped to distract the Sun King
from any militaristic ambitions he might have towards
Germany. Nothing came of that – although Napoleon
would invade Egypt in 1798 using tactics similar to those
devised by Leibniz over a century earlier. However, Leibniz
took the opportunity to meet with all the luminaries in
the foremost city of culture in Europe. He started studying
mathematics, quickly becoming one of the foremost
mathematicians in the world, and making a number of
important discoveries, including the famous differential
calculus. He also proudly showed off an extraordinary
mechanical calculator he had built, over a century and a

half before the more celebrated work of Charles Babbage.

In fact, Leibniz's interests were so wide-ranging that he could never keep his mind on what he was meant to be doing. In 1676, he became Court Chancellor of Hanover, and was put in charge of the court library. But he was more interested in the Harz mines, and spent years devising increasingly ingenious devices to solve the problem of their drainage. His employers commissioned a history of their house from him, hoping to use it to reinforce their dynastic claims over other German states. But Leibniz took the project far too seriously, beginning his research with the prehistory of the different nations of Europe, and becoming distracted by the important linguistic studies that this entailed. At the same time, he was working for several other German states, as well as the cities of Berlin and Vienna, for which he designed a number of worthy civic improvements. In his spare time, he was travelling endlessly around Europe, meeting other stalwarts of the Age of Reason, and carrying out his work in mathematics, chemistry, physics, metaphysics and theology. He produced hardly any books of importance, but his vast correspondence, much of which is still in the process of being edited and published, dwarfed the output of most of his contemporaries; and there cannot have been any subject, however obscure, with which he did not deal, and on which he was not an authority. Leibniz died in 1716, an increasingly marginalized figure, defiantly wearing his long brocade coat and huge wig which had gone out of style some decades earlier, and still working on his interminable royal histories, which he had hoped to complete before getting down to some serious philosophical work.

Despite Leibniz's pre-eminence in intellectual circles, it was not until the eighteenth century that the German Enlightenment really got into gear, and even so it continued to lag behind France and Britain. The largest of the German states, Prussia, took the leading role, as its rulers sought to drag their country into the modern age.

'Minds are also images of the Deity or Author of nature Himself, capable of knowing the system of the universe, and to some extent of imitating it.'

GOTTFRIED LEIBNIZ,
MONADOLOGY 83

Frederick Wilhelm, who came to the Prussian throne in 1713, began the process by reforming the country's economy – having learnt valuable lessons while staying with his relatives in the Netherlands.

Frederick Wilhelm, a fastidious Lutheran, had no love for Catholic France, but his son, Frederick II, the Great,

The Russian Enlightenment

He is a man of very hot temper, soon inflamed and very brutal in his passion. He raises his natural heat by drinking much brandy, which he rectifies himself with great application. He is subject to convulsive motions all over his body, and his head seems to be affected with these. He wants not capacity, and has a larger measure of knowledge than might be expected from his education, which was very indifferent. A want of judgment, with an instability of temper, appear in him too often and too evidently.

That was Bishop Burnet's judgment when, in England in 1698, he met Peter the Great, recently enthroned as the Tsar of all Russia. The bad-tempered alcoholic whom Burnet described, however, was engaged on an audacious mission, travelling throughout western Europe, learning everything he could about Enlightenment culture, economics and engineering. His plan was to drag Russia into the modern world.

Although Russia was, geographically, in Europe – or at least part of it was – it had for some centuries been quite isolated. It had been ruled by the oriental Mongols for much of the late Middle Ages, and it was the bastion of Orthodox Christianity, a separate denomination from the Catholics and Protestants in the West. Westerners knew virtually nothing about Russian religion, and Russians cared virtually nothing for western religion.

So it is hardly surprising that, when Peter returned home, he had to enforce his westernizing reforms with an iron hand in order to make any headway. The wearing of beards – a revered symbol of Orthodoxy – was banned, in an attempt to get people to look more western. Young men were happy to comply, as the women preferred it – but many old men kept their beards in boxes, fearing that they could not be saved without them. Traditional Russian dress, reaching down to the ankle, was banned: everyone had to dress like the French, and anyone who refused had their clothes cut down to size. English hairstyles were mandatory for women. Schools were built, the calendar reformed, military conscription introduced, and the church hierarchy placed firmly under state control. Like Louis XIV's France, Peter's was a quite different kettle of fish. Upon his accession to the throne in 1740, he immediately set about building upon his father's practical reforms with a determined programme of cultural renovation. Among his first acts as ruler was to recall from exile Christian Wolff, the leading German philosopher and Leibniz's natural heir, who had

The State Hermitage Museum, St Petersburg.

Russia was an avowedly Christian country. As a symbol of the new, western Russia, Peter transferred the capital to a new city, St Petersburg, on the Baltic coast.

Peter was hardly a model of Enlightenment tolerance – in 1718, he had his own son tortured to death for treason. But his reforms were extended and completed by Catherine the Great, a Prussian who became Empress of Russia in 1762 by organizing a coup against her own husband. Unlike Peter, Catherine had grown up in western Europe and thoroughly imbibed the principles of the Enlightenment. She corresponded with Voltaire, d'Alembert and other leading cultural figures, and patronized the arts generously, founding the famous Hermitage Museum in St Petersburg. Catherine was also an enormously skilled diplomat, and as the most powerful monarch in Europe extended Russian influence throughout the continent.

been expelled from the country by the humourless and disapproving Frederick Wilhelm. Equally radical was Frederick II's enthusiasm for French culture. French was spoken at his court, and it was at his invitation that Voltaire moved to Prussia in 1749. Frederick was also keen to bolster the position of Prussia in Europe, which he did by engaging in a series of wars between the 1740s and 1760s.

The new world

It should be fairly clear now that the Enlightenment was essentially a European movement. It had a great effect on one other continent, however – North America, an immense area blessed with rich natural resources. Enormous swathes of land there had been claimed by the various European powers during the century after they discovered it in 1497, but wars and other distractions in Europe had meant that there had been little attempt to back up these claims with colonizing. The supposedly largely empty land was thus an irresistible magnet to those fleeing persecution, or seeking adventure, and throughout the seventeenth century there was a steady and increasing stream of emigration from Europe to the new lands. It was here that, in 1620, the Pilgrim Fathers arrived, having fled persecution against the Puritans in England. The rigorous Calvinist state that they established in Massachusetts did not last long, although the religious and social principles on which it rested remained influential. Roger Williams, a clergyman who protested against the Puritan form of government, set up the colony of Providence in 1636, where the principle of the strict separation of church and state was first enacted in America. However, it was the Quakers who began importing some of the new social ideas coming from England, exemplified in the constitution of Pennsylvania in 1682, which guaranteed religious freedom for all.

By 1690 there were 250,000 Europeans living in North

America, and their number doubled every 25 years until there were over 2.5 million in 1775. By this time, there had developed a long-standing tradition that the colonies largely governed themselves, and there was increasing resentment towards the British Crown, which after the wars with France had gained control of most of the colonies. Not only that, but it benefited from their produce and, in the eyes of the colonists, cruelly oppressed them.

In their complaints against King George III, the colonists were enormously influenced by John Locke and his theories of government. The famous words of the Declaration of Independence, drafted by Thomas Jefferson in 1776, were essentially a restatement of Locke's philosophy:

We hold these truths to be self-evident, that all men are created equal, that they are endowed by their Creator with certain unalienable rights, that among these are life, liberty and the pursuit of happiness. That to secure these rights, governments are instituted among men, deriving their just powers from the consent of the governed, that whenever any form of government becomes destructive of these ends, it is the right of the people to alter or to abolish it, and to institute new government, laying its foundation on such principles and organizing its powers in such form, as to them shall seem most likely to effect their safety and happiness.

The conflict that followed ended in 1783 with the Treaty of Paris, at which Britain acknowledged the independence and right to self-government of the 13 United States of America. The new country had fought for its independence on the basis of Enlightenment ideals, and its new constitution was based on those same ideals.

The original World Wide Web
To the earnest scholars and scientists of the late seventeenth century, it must have seemed that there was

'Monarchy and succession have laid (not this or that kingdom only) but the world in blood and ashes... Of more worth is one honest man to society, and in the sight of God, than all the crowned ruffians that ever lived.'

THOMAS PAINE,
COMMON SENSE

no secret of nature too hard or profound for the human mind to uncover. A complete understanding of reality appeared within their grasp, and many hoped, accordingly, to organize and categorize this unprecedented body of knowledge. In essence, these scholars sought to create the nearest thing they could to the Internet.

The sheer audacity of this project could sometimes be quite breathtaking. No one, perhaps, was more ambitious than Leibniz. As a young man, his pioneering work in logic led him to believe that every statement about the world, however complex, can be broken down into simpler statements; and that all such statements, ultimately, are

A revolutionary philosopher

Portrait of Thomas Paine by John Wesley Jarvis, c. 1806.

The son of a Quaker, Thomas Paine was born in 1737 in Norfolk. An unsuccessful career as a tax officer ended in 1774 when he met Benjamin Franklin, who recommended that he emigrate to America.

Arriving in Philadelphia, Paine quickly latched onto the growing revolutionary mood in the colonies and became known as one of the most radical thinkers around. His *African Slavery in America* of 1775 attacked the now long-established practice of slavery in the colonies, and the following year he published his famous *Common Sense*, setting out the grounds for complete independence from England. He extended the theories of John Locke to argue that government was a necessary evil, the function of which was simple regulation, and which was best kept in check by representation. However, there was nothing representative about being made up of a finite number of perfectly simple concepts. The organization of knowledge would therefore be the simple, if lengthy, process of assigning a symbol to each of these concepts and setting them out. Incredibly, Leibniz believed that once this was done there would be no more disputes about any subject under the sun. If two people disagreed on any matter, they would simply set out the concepts involved and say, 'Let us calculate.'

Needless to say, Leibniz did not get very far with this project, and while he wrote several introductions to his projected encyclopedia of all knowledge, he never got around to the minor task of actually compiling the thing.

a colony of a country on the other side of the world. The book sold half a million copies.

Paine returned to England in 1787, but quickly became closely involved in the French Revolution. He supported the Revolutionaries with *The Rights of Man* of 1791, a book which was banned in England for its hostility to the notion of monarchy. The orthodox Anglican philosopher William Paley once found a copy in his house, and promptly hurled it into the fire.

It was followed up by the equally famous *Age of Reason*, published in 1793, which not only praised the age in which Paine lived but gave it a name. Most of the book was devoted to demonstrating the absurdity of the supposition that God's word could exist in written form, and the particular absurdity of the doctrine of the inspiration of the Bible. Paine, however, was in French prison when the book came out, having shown a touch of uncharacteristic moderation by voting against the execution of King Louis XVI. Paine returned to America in 1802, where he found that he was now viewed as an infidel and an atheist, and where he died seven years later.

Indeed, later in life he abandoned even the principle of universal comprehensibility and codification which underlay it.

Other writers of the period, however, kept their aims a little more modest, and enjoyed considerable success. The supreme example from the seventeenth century was Pierre Bayle's *Historical and Critical Dictionary*, perhaps the single most important work of the early part of the Enlightenment. Bayle was a Frenchman, the son of a Protestant minister, who in his youth had converted to Catholicism, benefited from the education offered by the Jesuits, and then promptly converted back to the Reformed Church. His outspoken views on religious freedom and tolerance meant that he spent most of his life in the Netherlands, where he worked on his *Dictionary*, which appeared in 1696. Bayle sought to create the definitive reference work on all philosophical and theological movements and thinkers, but much of the interest of his book lay not in the entries themselves but in the wittily sceptical footnotes with which he adorned them. The appearance of the *Dictionary* is a jumbled mess, with the articles surrounded not only by voluminous footnotes but by marginal inscriptions and cross-references; but this treasure trove of information was enormously popular throughout the eighteenth century. Philosophers and men of letters would pore through its pages for inspiration or support.

This categorizing ideal, the notion that order could be brought to the realms of human knowledge and to the world itself, produced other great projects too. The French Academy spent over half a century producing *The Dictionary of the French Academy*, published in 1694, a minute survey of the meanings and derivations of French words. Inspired by this, a group of English publishers commissioned Dr Samuel Johnson, at that time a hack for hire but later to become one of the leading savants of eighteenth-century England, to do the same for their language. *The Dictionary of the English Language* duly appeared in 1755. It was the product of 12 years' work by one of the most gifted writers of all time, and undoubtedly the most famous work of lexicography and etymology ever produced.

An even more ambitious effort to bring all modern culture together onto a single bookshelf was initiated by Denis Diderot, another Frenchman, born in Langres in 1713. *Philosophe* supreme, Diderot embodied the Enlightenment ideal of polymath virtuosity, being a linguist, man of letters, mathematician and philosopher; and like d'Holbach he was something of a radical, having abandoned Christianity not for enlightened deism but for rationalist atheism. Indeed, in 1749 he was imprisoned for his materialist views, including a kind of proto-Darwinist belief that living things had evolved by adapting, rather than being created by God. Diderot spent much of his life on the run, although Catherine the Great of Russia did buy his books from him to keep them safe.

In 1745 he was engaged to translate an English encyclopedia into French, but he revised it to such an extent that he created an entirely new work. At first he co-edited the project with the *philosophe* and scientist Jean d'Alembert, but later Diderot took over the work alone. The *Encyclopedia* finally appeared in 17 volumes, with a further 11 volumes of illustrations, between 1751 and 1772. It was written by Diderot himself and a team of thinkers drawn from all walks of life, united by their faith in the powers of human reason and their unremitting opposition to the forces of reaction and tradition, wherever they might be found. Needless to say, the *Encyclopedia* drew a barrage of attacks from both church and state, and the later volumes had to be published surreptitiously; but the project was an enormous success. It was widely read by all levels of educated society – not just aristocrats, but lawyers and even priests – even though all these people were bitterly attacked in its pages. Because it was written by so many people, including all of the leading *philosophes*, Diderot's *Encyclopedia* was *the*

'Reason is the great distinction of human nature, the faculty by which we approach the same degree of association with celestial intelligences.'

SAMUEL JOHNSON, *RAMBLER*, ISSUE 162

central text of the French Enlightenment. It played a major role in disseminating Enlightenment ideals of tolerance, reason and progress around Europe. Thus, it occupied a similar sort of role in the late Enlightenment to that of Bayle's *Dictionary* in the early Enlightenment – the Bible of the Age of Reason.

The New Science

The seeds that people such as Francis Bacon and Paracelsus had planted in the Renaissance came to fruition in the Enlightenment. Where they had attributed the properties of natural objects to the operation of spirits or the action of 'virtues', however, their successors were beginning to propose physical, quantifiable explanations for natural phenomena. And where the Renaissance savants had called their discipline 'magic', it was now turning into 'science'.

The basic belief that powered this transformation was that the world was fundamentally comprehensible. There was still a place, perhaps, for 'magic' in the sense of the art of manipulating and controlling nature: after all, perhaps astrology was true, in which case it could be studied scientifically. Descartes himself, who rejected the occult 'virtues' of Paracelsus and his ilk, believed that his philosophy could provide a rational explanation of how magic worked, and some of his disciples tried to do just that. But 'magic' in the sense of mysterious forces that defy explanation was given short shrift.

During this century and a half, science progressed further, perhaps, than it had during the preceding millennium. It was an exciting time, at least for those involved, and it must have seemed to many that humanity was on the threshold of uncovering all the secrets of the universe. To others, of course, the enterprise was incomprehensible or even comic, and the satirist Jonathan Swift mocked the new scientific societies and their members in his *Gulliver's Travels* of 1726.

'When a distinguished but elderly scientist states that something is possible, he is almost certainly right. When he states that something is impossible, he is very probably wrong.'

ARTHUR C. CLARKE,
PROFILES OF THE FUTURE

The new astronomy
It was in 1632 that Galileo published his *Dialogue*

Gulliver visits the 'Academy of Lagado'

The first man I saw was of a meagre aspect, with sooty hands and face, his hair and beard long, ragged and singed in several places. His clothes, shirt and skin were all of the same colour. He had been eight years upon a project for extracting sunbeams out of cucumbers, which were to be put into vials hermetically sealed, and let out to warm the air in raw inclement summers. He told me he did not doubt in eight years more he should be able to supply the governor's gardens with sunshine at a reasonable rate; but he complained that his stock was low, and entreated me to give him something as an encouragement to ingenuity, especially since this had been a very dear season for cucumbers. I made him a small present, for my lord had furnished me with money on purpose, because he knew their practice of begging from all who go to see them.

I went into another chamber, but was ready to hasten back, being almost overcome with a horrible stink… The projector of this cell was the most ancient student of the Academy. His face and beard were of a pale yellow; his hands and clothes daubed over with filth. When I was presented to him, he gave me a close embrace (a compliment I could well have excused). His employment from his first coming into the Academy, was an operation to reduce human excrement to its original food, by separating the several parts, removing the tincture which it receives from the gall, making the odour exhale, and scumming off the saliva…

I saw another at work to calcine ice into gunpowder; who likewise showed me a Treatise he had written concerning the malleability of fire, which he intended to publish.

GULLIVER'S TRAVELS PART 3, CHAPTER 5

Enlightenment man himself becomes an object of scrutiny to the giant scholars of Lorbruldrud in *Gulliver's Travels*. Late nineteenth-century illustration in *The Coloured Picture Book for the Nursery.*

Concerning the Two Chief World Systems, which drew the ire of the Inquisition. Yet Galileo was the shape of things to come. The century that followed would see perhaps the most audacious advances in humanity's understanding of the universe until the dawning of the space age.

One of the main spurs to the new discoveries was the telescope. Galileo had invented a much improved version of the primitive instruments that existed in his time, and used it to examine the surface of the moon, the satellites of Jupiter, and much else. In 1632, the first observatory was built in Leiden, in Holland, and five years later Copenhagen established the first national observatory. Across Europe, amateurs and professionals alike were scrutinizing the heavens on a previously unheard of scale.

One of the most obvious objects in the sky to point a telescope at is the moon, and indeed it was in 1647 that Johannes Hevelius published the first map of the moon. Hevelius was a wealthy Polish amateur who built his own observatory in the attic and, being blessed with exceptional eyesight, refused to use a telescope when working out the positions of stars (although he did build a number of huge telescopes for other astronomical observations). In 1651, another map of the moon was published by John Baptist Riccioli. Riccioli was a Jesuit, and had actually been commissioned by the Jesuits to examine Galileo's theories and refute them. Riccioli was a careful and thorough scientist, and as a Jesuit he had access to a lot of data that Galileo did not know – the Jesuits had sent missionaries all over the world, from South America to West Africa to Japan, and the scientifically inclined ones were bringing back observations of celestial phenomena that could not be seen from Europe. As a good Catholic, Riccioli concluded that Galileo was wrong, and the old Ptolemaic system was indeed true. But he did believe that the Copernican theory was a reasonable scientific hypothesis, one which simply happened to turn out to be false when tested. Of course, on this matter Riccioli was wrong, but in his outlook and methodology, he was very modern. He rejected Galileo not

'I think that in the discussion of natural problems we ought to begin not with the Scriptures, but with experiments, and demonstrations.'

GALILEO GALILEI,
THE AUTHORITY OF SCRIPTURE IN PHILOSOPHICAL CONTROVERSIES

on the basis of tradition or dogma, as the Inquisition had; rather, he subjected his theory to proper scientific testing. In his understanding of science as the proposing and testing of hypotheses, which are to be received or rejected on the basis of the evidence, Riccioli is the model of modern scientific method. It is fitting that the names he gave to features on the moon's surface are still used today.

However, it was quickly becoming clear that Copernicus and Galileo had been right. Galileo had proved that not every celestial body revolves around the earth, because he had been the first to observe the moons of Jupiter. Now others were turning their attention to the planets. The Dutch astronomer Christian Huygens discovered Titan, Saturn's largest moon, as well as the rings of Saturn – which Galileo had seen without realizing what they were. In 1659, Huygens was the first to describe the patterns on the surface of Mars. Seven years later, the French scientist Jean Cassini observed the Martian polar ice caps for the first time.

An outstanding figure in the next generation of astronomers was the Englishman John Flamsteed. As a youth, Flamsteed had been too sickly to go to university, and had been forced to teach himself science – in the face of fierce opposition from his father, who feared that it would ruin his son's health completely. Nevertheless, Flamsteed succeeded in gaining the attention of the scientific community, and in 1675 King Charles II appointed

'The world is my country, and science is my religion.'

CHRISTIAN HUYGENS

him the first Astronomer Royal. Flamsteed set up his observatory in Greenwich, in east London, and proceeded to map the heavens to a degree of accuracy never before seen. Flamsteed was the kind of man who never makes any exciting and world-shattering discovery, but who is essential to the progress of science: a patient data-gatherer, whose observations can be used to support the new ideas of great thinkers such as his contemporary

Lithograph of Galileo Galilei demonstrating his telescope.

Sir Isaac Newton. Newton, for one, was well aware of this, and spent much time coaxing Flamsteed into giving him the information he required to construct his theories. Unfortunately, Flamsteed does not seem to have understood what Newton needed, and the two of them did not get on at all well. In fact, Flamsteed was an exceptionally bitter and unpleasant person. He engaged in a fierce controversy with Hevelius over whether telescopes should be used in determining stellar positions, but most of his vitriol was reserved for Sir Edmund Halley, a man he loathed with a burning passion.

Halley, for his part, was a true seventeenth-century scientific adventurer. He attended The Queen's College, Oxford, but in 1676 gave up his studies in order to sail to St Helena and map the southern stars. During the voyage he also experimented with diving bells, which he believed were the key to the future exploration of the ocean's depths. On his return, Halley expanded his interests to geology, oceanography and mathematics as well as astronomy, and won serious acclaim – although the opposition of Flamsteed hampered him. One reason Flamsteed hated Halley was that the younger man had, without his permission, published some of his observations prematurely, since Newton and others desperately needed them. Another reason was that Halley was suspected of denying the truth of the biblical creation story – a charge that Halley denied, but to no avail. Nevertheless, when Flamsteed died in 1720, Halley succeeded him as Astronomer Royal. Flamsteed's widow saw to it that her husband's instruments were all sold, so that Halley would never use them.

Despite all this, Halley's fame rests on his observations of a spectacular comet that passed Europe in 1682. Halley knew that a similar comet had been seen in 1607, and earlier another one in 1531. He realized that they were all the same comet, returning every 76 years, and predicted that it would be seen again in 1758. It was a monumental piece of work, simply because comets had

Detail from the Bayeux Tapestry of man-at-arms warning Harold II of the disastrous omen heralded by the appearance of Halley's Comet (upper left).

always been so strange and unpredictable. They had been interpreted as omens – hence the prominence of a comet depicted in the Bayeaux Tapestry, warning of the Norman invasion of 1066. And these attitudes were still common even in Halley's time: Pierre Bayle had ridiculed them in his *Thoughts on the Comet* of 1680, in which he had argued that comets must be regular phenomena like everything else. Thus, there was considerable acclaim for Halley when his comet duly returned at exactly the time the great man had predicted, 15 years after his death. Even the famous comet of 1066 had been nothing other than an earlier appearance of Halley's Comet.

Newton and the secrets of the universe

Without a doubt, however, the greatest scientist of the Age of Reason, and the man popularly regarded as the greatest Englishman of his age, was Sir Isaac Newton. Appropriately enough, given the almost messianic status he was later to hold, Newton was born on Christmas Day 1642 in Lincolnshire. After an unhappy childhood and an indifferent career at school, Newton succeeded in entering

Trinity College, Cambridge, in 1661 – where, like other students who were not well off, he paid part of his expenses by acting as a servant to richer students. Although he was meant to be studying law, he discovered mathematics and quickly devoured all the books he could find on the subject. In 1665, the university was forced to close because of the plague, and Newton returned to Lincolnshire for two years. Here, apparently purely for his own entertainment, he made most of his groundbreaking mathematical discoveries, including the 'method of fluxions', which anticipated Leibniz's differential calculus by some years. It was also here that, according to legend, Newton saw an apple fall off a tree and wondered what made things go down.

In 1667, after the university reopened, Newton returned to Cambridge and became a Fellow. His discoveries were still largely unknown, although some of his ideas did start to spread by word of mouth. Unable to take criticism, the shy and sensitive Newton continued his policy of hardly ever publishing anything, and indeed in 1678 he seems to have suffered something of a nervous breakdown and withdrew further into his shell.

Newton's greatest work at this time was undoubtedly his research into gravitation. He had realized that the force which pulled an apple to the ground might be the same one that kept the moon revolving around the earth. He could explain much of the motions of celestial objects by mathematical rules he had deduced during his sabbatical in Lincolnshire, including the rules of centrifugal force, which tends to fling an orbiting body away from the thing it is orbiting. Newton calculated that an orbiting body is kept in place by a combination of this centrifugal force and the force of gravity, which attracts it to the thing it is orbiting; furthermore, he deduced the 'inverse square law' of gravity, which states that the gravitational force between two objects varies by the reverse of the square of their distance.

Some other members of the Royal Society were also

'I do not know what I may appear to the world; but to myself I seem to have been only like a boy playing on the seashore, and diverting myself in now and then finding a smoother pebble or a prettier shell than ordinary, whilst the great ocean of truth lay all undiscovered before me.'

ISAAC NEWTON,
QUOTED IN
DAVID BREWSTER,
*MEMOIRS OF
NEWTON*

thinking along the same lines, including Halley, Robert Hooke and Sir Christopher Wren (who, despite his fame as an architect, was actually a mathematician and astronomer by profession). Astronomical observations had shown by this time that the planets move around the sun in ellipses, rather than in circles – another blow to the medieval system of thought, in which all celestial activities take place in circles. Halley and his colleagues were puzzled how to explain this, and in 1682, while having dinner with Newton, Halley asked him if he knew what path a planet would trace if it were governed by the inverse square law alone. Newton immediately replied that it would indeed be an ellipse. Astonished, Halley asked him how he knew. 'Why,' replied the mathematician, 'I have calculated it.' Halley asked to see the calculations, but a search of Newton's chaotic study revealed nothing. Newton promised to do the work again and send it to Halley, which he duly did. The astronomer was so excited that he insisted that Newton publish his findings.

In 1687, therefore, Newton produced – with Halley's financial help – the first volume of his *Mathematical Principles of Natural Philosophy* – or the *Principia*, as it is always known. It is generally recognized as the greatest scientific work ever published, in part because Newton successfully explained a whole variety of phenomena, from the motion of cannon balls to the tides of the sea, in terms of a few simple mathematical and physical laws – primarily the law of gravity. The mathematical rigour with which Newton presented his ideas made them essentially irrefutable, although it also made his book remarkably tough to read, which explains why it took a while for the scientific community to appreciate it. At this time, even in England, most people accepted the physics of Descartes, published some decades earlier. The physical world, according to Descartes, is made up of 'corpuscles', which are like tiny ball bearings, and all motion is caused by these corpuscles literally hitting into each other, like a chrome executive desk ornament. Different kinds of substance are simply made of corpuscles of different sizes or shapes, or moving at different speeds, and these differences are sufficient to explain, say, the different properties of water, iron and mercury, because the corpuscles themselves are all made of the same basic 'stuff'. So for Descartes the universe is like one of those toddlers' paddling pools filled with plastic balls that are sometimes found in amusement parks. The balls are, of course, too small to see, but everything can be explained

Robert Hooke

Not every scientist discovers a comet or a fundamental law of the universe – yet there is another, less dramatic kind of greatness. No Enlightenment scientist typified that more than Robert Hooke. His is not exactly a household name, perhaps partly because Sir Isaac Newton hated him and, even years after his death, would speak of him in the most unflattering way. Yet Hooke's wide-ranging studies, especially his use of the method of experiment, represent the ideal of Enlightenment science perfectly.

Robert Hooke was born on the Isle of Wight in 1635, and his youth was marred by unhappiness. He was physically and emotionally scarred by smallpox as a child, and was considered exceptionally ugly for the rest of his life; and when he was 13 his father hanged himself. He was always a loner, never marrying, despite an obsession with his own niece.

Nevertheless, Hooke succeeded in gaining a place at Oxford, where like Newton he worked as a servant to other students. Upon leaving university, his skill at setting up experiments landed him the role of assistant to the famous physicist Robert Boyle. In 1662, he became Curator of Experiments for the Royal Society, meaning that he was in charge of all demonstrations at meetings of the society. Since there were three or four experiments to carry out every week, and they could be on more or less any area of 'natural philosophy', Hooke had to become a master of every possible subject.

solely in terms of their movement. For example, in trying to explain why the planets revolve around the sun, Descartes developed his famous 'vortex' theory, according to which whirlpools of the tiny corpuscles that fill space whisk the planets (made of much bulkier corpuscles) along their orbits. In other words, the planets move because they are quite literally being pushed and sucked by the corpuscles that surround them.

Although his physics was easy to understand, Descartes had never really provided much evidence or

In the course of his experiments, Hooke made an enormous variety of discoveries, from geology to physics. He pioneered the study of fossils, which he argued were the remains of living creatures turned to stone by the action of mineral-rich water (as opposed to bizarre animal-shaped stones, as some others believed). He also argued that the geography of the earth had once been different, with the seas in different places, explaining the presence of fossils of marine creatures miles inland.

Hooke's most famous discoveries, however, were made with a sophisticated compound microscope of his own design, and were published in his celebrated *Micrographia* of 1665. This work featured descriptions and detailed drawings of tiny animals and plants, as revealed under the microscope. Among them was Hooke's account of what he saw when he looked at cork: a series of little boxes, which he called 'cells' because they reminded him of the rooms of a monastery.

Robert Hooke's microscope.

mathematical backing for it, and it was soon clear that Newton's alternative was much more satisfactory. Many, especially in France, were turned off by his apparent belief in action at a distance – after all, how can the earth act on the moon without touching it, and without any corpuscles between the two of them to communicate the action? For Newton, unlike Descartes, believed that space was a vacuum. One of the most cogent critics of Newton was Leibniz, who taught a more sophisticated version of Descartes' physics, and who pointed out that to say that objects attract each other because of their gravitational force doesn't explain anything. It is just restating the same fact in different words, like the old joke about the medieval philosopher who 'explained' that sleeping pills work because of their 'dormitive virtue'.

Leibniz had an axe to grind with Newton anyway – the bitter dispute, which continued to rage even after their deaths, over who had invented the differential calculus first. Newton himself was partly responsible for this squabble: as President of the Royal Society he had commissioned an 'impartial' investigation into the matter, the report of which he wrote himself, and which was not exactly flattering to his rival. In private, he had had no qualms about expressing his rage towards Leibniz, whom he regarded, quite unjustly, as a plagiarist of his work. In fact, it seems that Newton did think of it first, but Leibniz invented it independently and published first, and it is his version that is used today.

In 1693, Newton largely retired from scientific and mathematical research – apparently due, in part, to a recurrence of the depressive illness which seems to have dogged him throughout much of his life. He spent considerable energy on theological matters; like his friend Samuel Clarke, Newton's extensive study of the Bible led him to the conclusion that the orthodox doctrine of the Trinity was not to be found in it, and that Christ was therefore not God but simply the most exalted of God's creatures. This notion, a reformulation of the ancient

'When I wrote my treatise about our system, I had an eye upon such principles as might work with considering men for the belief of a Deity; and nothing can rejoice me more than to find it useful for that purpose.'

ISAAC NEWTON,
LETTER TO BENTLEY
1692

Arian heresy, was naturally highly controversial. Newton was wise to keep fairly quiet about it, unlike Clarke, who endured many years in controversy. Newton was also interested in alchemy and devoted much time to the attempt to turn base materials into gold – which shows the extent to which Renaissance ideas and practices were still influential, even to the greatest scientist of the age. Today, we regard alchemy as a superstitious 'pseudo-science', but in Newton's day it was still a legitimate scientific pursuit, because it had not yet been shown to be false.

Newton, who was fiercely Protestant and resented the Catholic policies of King James II, was a member of the parliament that, in 1688, offered the crown to William of Orange. William reciprocated in 1696 when he made Newton the first Warden of the Mint, clearly recognizing that England's foremost mathematical genius was the man for the job. In 1705 Newton became the first person

'Nature and nature's laws lay hid from sight. God said, Let Newton be! And all was light.'

ALEXANDER POPE, *EPITAPH FOR SIR ISAAC NEWTON,* 1727

Newton by **William Blake, 1795.**

to be knighted for his services to science. Between then
and his death in 1727, his reputation was assured as the
greatest genius England had ever produced, a colossus
of the Age of Reason. That the scientific community
could pass, in less than a century, from the condemnation
of Galileo to the apotheosis of Newton is a striking
illustration of the progress and changes in thinking
that the Enlightenment had brought about.

Medicine and biology

While the astronomers and physicists were laying bare
the fundamental laws of the universe, anatomists and
physicians were discovering whole new worlds within.
The groundwork for the new discoveries had been laid by
anatomists such as Sir William Harvey, a former student
of Francis Bacon, who rose to become personal physician
to King James I. Harvey had published, in 1628, the book
which would make him famous – *On the Motion of the
Heart and Blood in Animals* – in which he set out his
theory of the circulation of the blood, overturning
accepted theories on the functions of the heart and lungs
that had held sway for centuries. There was a veritable
craze for anatomical research at this time, and it was part
of the Enlightenment ideal of learning by studying the
world itself, rather than the books of authorities from the
past. Harvey had exemplified this ideal in his book on the
circulation of the blood, where he set out the theories
of earlier authorities and then demolished them by
describing simple experiments and observations.

Something of the spirit of enlightened enquiry which
the study of anatomy represented to seventeenth-century
scientists comes across in Rembrandt's *The Anatomy
Lesson of Dr Nicolaes Tulp*, painted in 1632. Even René
Descartes, a man popularly conceived as a 'rationalist'
philosopher who spent his days dreaming up metaphysical
theories while warming his hands before a stove, was in
the habit of buying carcasses from butchers' shops and
devoting considerable time to dissecting them. There is a

The world of inner space

In an age when science was becoming the increasing preserve of the professional, when aristocrats formed scientific societies and enjoyed royal patronage, Antony van Leeuwenhoek was something of a throwback to a more carefree time. He belonged to the artisan class, and indeed spent most of his life as a draper, although he also worked in a variety of other jobs. He didn't even know any French or Latin, which might have helped communicate his ideas to other scientists.

Fortunately, other scientists recognized the importance of this Dutch amateur's work anyway. Leeuwenhoek spent much of his spare time grinding lenses, which he fashioned into simple microscopes. In fact, his designs were extremely simple, consisting of a single lens on a handle, and so were more like magnifying glasses than the more

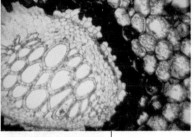

sophisticated instruments used by contemporaries such as Robert Hooke. However, they were more powerful, and Leeuwenhoek was blessed with excellent vision.

With the zeal of the true scientific pioneer, Leeuwenhoek used his lenses to scrutinize virtually everything he could lay hands on, however mundane or revolting, from fossils to bee stings, and even the saliva of two old men who had never cleaned their teeth in their lives. Leeuwenhoek's observations of the latter produced the first description of bacteria, and we can only imagine the draper's amazement as, seemingly everywhere he looked, he discovered further incredible worlds of living creatures too small to see with the naked eye. He described his discoveries in letters to the British Royal Society, which eventually elected him a member, although he never attended a meeting. By the time of his death in 1723, he was recognized as one of the most important scientific discoverers of his age.

Light micrograph of a tranverse section of the Royal fern, *Osmunda*, photographed through a Leeuwenhoek single-lensed microscope. Magnification x 375.

story of a visitor who, on entering Descartes' study, was shocked to find him covered in gore, working on a dead horse. 'Monsieur Descartes,' he gasped, 'where are your books?' 'Why, Monsieur,' replied the philosopher, indicating the entrails with which he was surrounded, 'here is my library!'

Despite the relative roughness and crudity, by modern standards, of the medical advances of the Age of Reason, they changed the world to such a degree that it is almost impossible for us to imagine the time before them. Perhaps the greatest advance of all was made by a

The Anatomy Lecture of Dr Nicolaes Tulp by Rembrandt, 1632.

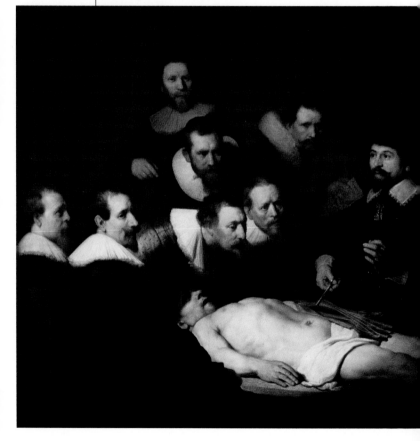

or named Edward Jenner, who in
first smallpox vaccine. Since between
all deaths were caused by smallpox,
ed above all others – far more, even,
today – as the greatest scourge
ner dreamed that one day his
e, which made patients immune to
the much milder cowpox, might
entirely – a dream which must have
otimistic at the time. However, his
ne true in 1980, which means that
Jenner was probably responsible for
saving more lives than anyone else
in history.

At the same time, a quiet
revolution in anatomy was being
undertaken by the Italian Marcello
Malpighi, who rose to become
personal physician to Pope
Innocent XII at the end of the
seventeenth century. Malpighi was
one of the first to use microscopes
to further the study of anatomy,
and he made an enormous variety
of discoveries in this way – most
famously discovering the tiny
blood vessels called capillaries.
Malpighi was also a taxonomist
and did groundbreaking work on
the categorizing of living things
on the basis of their internal
structure.

This was quite a revolutionary
endeavour, as we can appreciate if
we think back to the Renaissance
world view typified by Paracelsus,
who characterized plants solely by
their degrees of usefulness to

*'Future nations
will know by
history only that
the loathsome
smallpox has
existed and by
you has been
extirpated.'*

THOMAS JEFFERSON,
*LETTER TO EDWARD
JENNER*

humans. And this view of nature – interesting only inasmuch as it relates to us – came across in the work of naturalists such as Conrad Gesner, possibly the greatest biologist of the sixteenth century, who in the 1550s published his *History of Animals*. This was essentially a compendium of every fact Gesner could lay his hands on about each creature – whether culled from scientific observations or from folk wisdom. And how does Gesner classify his entries? Simple – in alphabetical order of their Latin names.

This approach, which seems so unscientific to us today, was still alive and well in 1616, when the Italian naturalist Ulysse Aldrovandi's posthumous *History of Quadrupeds* appeared. Aldrovandi started his work with the horse, stating that the reason for this was that it is the most useful animal to man; and his treatment of each animal features not only what we would recognize as scientific description, but also notes on the husbandry and care of the various creatures. Like Gesner's earlier work, it is a fascinating treasure trove of information and anecdote, but one that categorizes animals only by features that are of direct interest to human beings.

Clearly, Malpighi's attempt to categorize living things on the basis of their intrinsic features – even internal features, normally of no interest to human beings – was a major move away from this kind of approach. It was a move away from thinking of the world only as the stage on which human beings made their entrances and exits, and one towards thinking of the world as an objective entity in its own right, one in which human beings have a place, certainly, but one in which other things are intrinsically interesting too.

Undoubtedly the most important figure in the change to this new way of understanding the world was the Swedish naturalist Carl von Linné, normally known by his Latinized name, Carolus Linnaeus. Linnaeus's father was a Lutheran pastor, and hoped that his son, born in 1707, would follow in his footsteps; unfortunately, he

'As soon as men had persuaded themselves that all things which were made, were made for their sakes, they were bound to consider as most important in everything that which was the most useful to them.'

BARUCH DE SPINOZA,
ETHICS I APPENDIX

showed no interest in the church, and instead went to the University of Lund to study medicine. Part of this involved the study of botany, to train the medics in herbal remedies, just as Paracelsus had recommended centuries earlier; and this fuelled a fascination with plants that Linnaeus had shown from a young age. Indeed, Linnaeus interrupted his studies to visit central Sweden and Lapland on specimen-gathering expeditions.

Linnaeus became a professor at Uppsala University in 1741, where he promptly rearranged the university's botanical garden and started sending students out on more specimen-gathering expeditions. These expeditions would, eventually, take his students all over the known world and beyond: one accompanied Captain James Cook on his voyage of discovery in the southern hemisphere.

It was on the basis of the growing collection and his studies of it that Linnaeus produced his *System of Nature*, published in 1735 and revised over the following decades. In it, Linnaeus proposed a new way of naming and ordering living things. Like Malpighi, he sought to do this solely on the basis of the structures of organisms themselves, rather than on anything to do with their relation to human beings. The most famous example of this approach was his reclassification of plants based on the numbers of stamens and pistils found in their flowers – a rather shocking thing at the time, since these were structures used in sexual reproduction!

Linnaeus believed that the basic 'building block' of the natural world was the species. Every living thing was a member of one, and only one, species. But each species also belonged to a genus – a higher classification and one which was also based on structural similarities. At higher levels still, genera were grouped into orders, orders into classes and, finally, classes into kingdoms. And Linnaeus invented a new way of referring to each species: the 'binomial classification', according to which the genus is given first, followed by the species. Human beings, therefore, are '*Homo sapiens*' – 'the wise species of the human genus' – a description that many have questioned since.

Although Linnaeus had never wanted to enter the church, he had a deeply religious outlook on the world. He believed that the classification he described was not simply an arbitrary way of dividing up the natural world imposed by our own minds for our own convenience,

The cabinet of curiosities

The cabinet of curiosities was the physical manifestation of the Renaissance and Enlightenment ideal to learn from nature itself rather than from books. Men of science naturally collected interesting objects to study, and by the eighteenth century a 'cabinet of curiosities' was quite a fashionable feature of many aristocratic homes throughout Europe. People vied with each other in collecting the most exotic or repulsive objects available – grotesquely mutated animals were particularly highly prized. While these had good shock value, such one-offs rather went against the basic ideology underlying the cabinet of curiosities, which was classification. The collectors were essentially creating three-dimensional versions of the encyclopedias and dictionaries that were becoming such a feature of the Age of Reason. They sought to bring together the whole of nature – as far as possible – under one roof, and there to sort, describe and classify it all.

In the hands of true aficionados, these collections could easily outgrow the cabinets in which they were originally kept. One of the largest and most famous collections belonged to an Amsterdam pharmacist named Albertus Seba, who possessed a vast array of strange creatures and plants from around the world, including, we are assured, a hydra and a dragon. In 1731 he published a beautifully illustrated catalogue of his collection. It ran into four volumes.

Inevitably, collections on this scale could outgrow the means of private individuals, and many cabinets of curiosities would form the nucleus of nineteenth- and twentieth-century museums. These museums, which combined the scientific ideals of the cabinets with the additional aim of educating the general public, were also anticipated in the Age of Reason. Enlightened monarchs maintained special cabinets for public edification. When Peter the Great opened his in St Petersburg in 1714, he declared, 'I want the people to look and learn.'

like listing things in alphabetical order. On the contrary, it was a real and objective structure of reality, which had been established by God himself. For Linnaeus, science and theology merged to form a single body of knowledge, one whose ultimate subject was not the world but God. It was a notion of science that had its roots in the Middle Ages, and one that would continue

Spiders and snakes from Albertus Seba's *Locupletissimi Rerum Naturalium*, 1750. Hand coloured engraving.

to exercise a powerful sway well into the nineteenth century. But as we shall see, it was one that was already being determinedly undermined by Enlightenment thinkers themselves.

The Churches

The Age of Reason was at once a time of great danger and an unparalleled opportunity for the Christian churches of Europe. On the one hand, the scientists were busy demolishing much of the cherished world view of the Middle Ages and the Reformation, and on the other, the philosophers were equally busy building a new one. To conservative factions, in all the churches, the old ways of thinking were part and parcel of their religion, and the whole thing seemed to be under threat. But more progressive Christians realized that the changing times offered Christianity new ideas and new world views, which might prove profitable allies.

The Catholic Church

The Age of Reason was not a great time for the Church of Rome, at least in Europe. The extraordinary gains that the Protestant churches had made throughout Europe in the sixteenth century seemed, by the seventeenth, to have ended. But all sides were now forced to recognize that no single church would ever again have unchallenged dominion over Europe, as the Treaty of Westphalia made clear: every state could have whatever religion it liked. That was obviously a blow to Catholicism, as it was to the other denominations; but at least the Catholic Church had a secret weapon in the form of the Jesuits. This society had been founded along military lines in 1540 by a soldier named Ignatius Loyola, and it was enormously successful in persecuting heresy at home and spreading the gospel abroad. It was partly due to the efforts of the Jesuits that, by the end of the Thirty Years War, Catholicism was firmly entrenched throughout most of southern Europe, including Spain, France, Italy and the southern German

'Man is created to praise, reverence and serve God our Lord, and by this means to save his soul.'

IGNATIUS OF LOYOLA, *SPIRITUAL EXERCISES* I.1

states. The failure of the Jesuit missions in the Far East – Japan had banned Christianity in 1614 – was compensated for by their continued success in South America.

At the same time, the papacy was gradually becoming increasingly impotent. The popes of the seventeenth century were not all perfect human beings, although some were decidedly saintly: there was still a lot of nepotism, the practice of conferring positions upon relatives, and the papacy still seemed to run in the family. But Pope Innocent XII did produce a papal bull ending the practice in 1692, and his successor, Clement XI, an enlightened man who patronized the arts and sciences, made great efforts to stamp it out. And the excesses of some of the notorious Renaissance popes, such as those in the Borgia family, had been consigned to history. Still, the Reformation had ended forever the position of the pope

Drawing of a mission and orchard by Father Florian Paucke, a Jesuit missionary who lived and worked with the Mocobi tribes of Chaco, South America.

as the most powerful prince in Europe. Even within his own church, the position of the pope was increasingly controversial. The notion of papal infallibility was a much debated topic by the seventeenth century, being increasingly promoted in Italy but resisted in France. It would not be declared a dogma of the church until the nineteenth century. For the most part, the Enlightenment saw the papacy becoming increasingly isolated from mainstream culture, and indeed to men such as Voltaire the papacy was the institution that represented par excellence the dogmatic, superstitious authoritarianism of the past, and the eternal enemy of reason and progress.

The Protestant churches

After the initial excitement of the Reformation died down, the Protestant churches went into a long period of retrenchment. This period, which lasted from the late sixteenth century to the late seventeenth, is often called the Age of Confessionalism – meaning that different groups became increasingly concerned with defining their own beliefs, or confessions, in contrast to everyone else's. It resulted in what is sometimes called 'Protestant scholasticism', as the churches dwelt to an increasingly sophisticated extent on their own doctrines, developing jargon to describe them more and more accurately – just as the medieval scholastics had done three centuries earlier.

Inevitably, the discussions became dry and technical. Luther had sought to overturn centuries of medieval definitions and jargon, and get back to the original message of the New Testament. Calvin is often thought of as a more 'systematic' theologian, but even his *Institutes of the Christian Religion*, carefully arranged by topic as it was, was intended to be no more than a faithful exposition of the Bible. Their heirs, however, were now going beyond this: while not abandoning the Protestant principle of the authority of scripture alone, they were seeking answers to questions not found in the Bible. The prime example was the issue of predestination and the relation between grace and free will – which, at the start of the seventeenth century, was the hot theological topic among Protestants and Catholics alike. A new kind of scholasticism was being produced, and some Protestant theologians were happy to use the terminology of Aristotle, and regarded Aquinas as an authority.

One of the key figures in this process was Theodore Beza, an aristocratic Frenchman who, although only ten years younger than Calvin, outlived him by 40 years and was widely regarded as the great man's natural successor. It was Beza, rather than Calvin, who was regarded by most Reformed theologians of the seventeenth century as *the* theological authority; and it was he who was especially good at recasting the terminology of Aristotle and the medieval scholastics in disputing with his opponents, both Lutheran and Catholic. And it was Beza who defined the doctrine of predestination and its role in Reformed theology. In so doing, he developed the doctrine of 'double predestination', the notion that God deliberately predestines some people – the reprobate – to damnation as well as others – the elect – to salvation. It was Beza, also, who put forward the 'prelapsarian' position, according to which God planned the fall and subsequent division of humankind into elect and reprobate even before Adam ate that fateful apple. These ideas were present, at least in germ, in Calvin, but they were not the touchstones of orthodoxy that they would later become.

Beza was a lively and elegant writer, but the same cannot be said of all of those who took up their pens in the service of the Lutheran and Reformed Churches. Logical consistency and adherence to a pre-established orthodoxy were fast becoming the watchwords, in place of the attempt simply to expound scripture that had marked Luther and Calvin.

Controversy

The Age of Confessionalism is often thought of as a time when theologians spent their time sharpening their pens against members of other churches, and it can be something of a surprise to discover that they all seemed to reserve their greatest bile for their own colleagues. In fact, the tension within the churches is quite understandable. With the hardening of orthodoxy, there were inevitable splits within the churches as some rebelled against what their colleagues were laying down as official doctrine. The greatest of these splits occurred in the Reformed Church at the end of the sixteenth century, after the preaching of Jacobus Arminius, a Dutch minister and professor who had been taught by Beza and was initially a supporter of his views. However, Arminius came to rebel against the doctrines of predestination and prelapsarianism, declaring them unjust: surely, he argued, if God condemns some and saves others, it must be on the basis of who has faith, not on the basis of some eternal decree he has already worked out even before they were born. Arminius died in 1609, but the controversy he had started rumbled on for decades. In 1618, the Dutch Reformed Church called the Synod of Dort to try to deal with it. The Canons of Dort that resulted form the classical 'Non-Remonstrant' statement of Calvinism, strongly upholding the doctrine of predestination.

And this sort of thing was not confined to Protestants. As we have seen, the Catholic Church was not a monolithic entity during this time, but a mixed bag of different groups and viewpoints. There too, there were internal disagreements. For example, in the late sixteenth and early seventeenth centuries there was a protracted row between the Jesuits and the Dominican friars over how divine grace and human free will interacted. A century later, Pope Innocent XI, who occupied the throne of St Peter from 1676 to 1689, spent almost all of his reign playing a power game with Louis XIV and the Gallican theologians such as Bossuet, who believed strongly in the authority of the Catholic Church, but not necessarily in that of the pope.

More serious was the rise of Jansenism. This movement grew out of an unlikely pairing: Cornelius

Jansen, professor of exegesis at Louvain University, and Jean Duvergier de Hauranne, a brilliant wit and spiritual director, who was Abbé de Saint-Cyran, by which name he is normally known. Saint-Cyran was a mentor to the nuns and male solitaries at the Abbey of Port-Royal near Paris, and it was here that the principles of Jansenism were nurtured and became notorious. Those principles were based on a book that Jansen published in 1640 entitled *Augustinus*, in which he tried to restate and defend what he believed were the doctrines of Augustine. In it, Jansen argued that divine grace can never be resisted, meaning that it always overrides the human will. He bitterly opposed the doctrine, associated with the Jesuits, that salvation depended on a kind of cooperation between divine grace and the human will. Thus, the Jansenists believed in predestination, which meant that although they were Catholics they were in some ways more like Calvinists.

Jansenism proved a thorn in the side of the Catholic Church, and especially the Jesuits, for some considerable time. Its leading exponent was Antoine Arnauld, an intellectual and cultural giant of the seventeenth century, who came from a large family, many of whom were also leading Jansenists. As a philosopher, Arnauld, who corresponded with such luminaries as Descartes, Malebranche and Leibniz, possessed a penetrating critical faculty; and as a theologian he was no less brilliant.

'Capacity for discerning the truth is the most important measure of minds.'

ANTOINE ARNAULD,
THE ART OF THINKING

The Church of England

The Anglican Church occupied a curious position in the midst of all this. On the one hand it was, historically, a Protestant church, having been created in the 1530s when King Henry VIII essentially took personal command of the existing Catholic Church in England. The Lutheran sympathies of his advisers, such as Thomas Cranmer and Thomas Cromwell, had influenced the new church, but so too did the Catholic tendencies of later monarchs such as Charles I and churchmen such as William Laud. The fact that, unlike other churches throughout Europe, the

The principles of the Church of England

The Church of England does not require a blind obedience; she is content her doctrines should be examined by the clearest light. Simplicity and truth seek not corners. The Holy Scriptures are allowed to the people, and no means of instruction wanting among us. She does not indeed vaunt of what she has not: she pretends not to any absolute infallibility. She is modest, and contains herself within due bounds, and withholds not from her children, either the liberty or means of examining her doctrines.

RICHARD KIDDER, BISHOP OF BATH AND WELLS (1691–1704), *THE JUDGEMENT OF PRIVATE DISCRETION IN MATTERS OF RELIGION DEFENDED*

Church of England rarely had to struggle for the souls of its nation with another church meant that it had never been forced to define its beliefs and practices very clearly in opposition to others. By the turn of the eighteenth century, the one thing that all Anglicans could agree on was a shared distrust of Roman Catholics.

This doctrinal openness meant that, as we shall see in subsequent chapters, it was in England that religious free-thinking had the greatest chance of taking root. In the late sixteenth century it was still possible to be burnt at the stake in England for denying the Trinity, but a century later those who asserted such things had no need to fear anything more damaging than parliamentary censure and an avalanche of refutations by the staunchly orthodox majority of Anglican clergy. For the Church of England prided itself on its doctrinal orthodoxy, understood in terms of common sense, and a middle way between what were regarded as the bizarre excesses of continental Protestants and Catholics. This middle way was based on what its practitioners felt was a healthy respect (but not *too* great a respect, which might border on idolatry) for tradition. This took shape in the principle of the apostolic succession, a very ancient Christian notion, according to which Christian doctrines can be known to be trustworthy because they are taught in churches which were founded by the apostles or their followers. In other words, great trust was placed in the notion of an unbroken chain of tradition going back to the apostles themselves. It was this 'apostolic succession', together with the scriptures, themselves handed down as part of this authoritative tradition, that mainstream Anglicans felt guaranteed the trustworthiness of their church. By contrast, many thought, the Catholics had added to that tradition over the centuries, while the more extreme Protestants had subtracted from it.

Ecumenical relations

There was considerable tension between the churches. The worst example was France, where after the Revocation of Nantes in 1685 the Protestants were an actively persecuted minority: they felt especially threatened by the encircling Catholics, and all the more determined never to give in to them. The persecutions only strengthened this resolve and inspired sympathy from Protestants throughout Europe, who by the same token became increasingly hostile to Catholicism. In England, by contrast, Catholicism was the minority faith: officially proscribed, its priests had to operate – to varying degrees – in secrecy. There is a story of Richard Challoner, vicar apostolic over Catholics in central England and North America – the equivalent of a bishop in what was designated mission territory – holding a Mass in an east London pub for a congregation of Irish workers disguised as beer-swilling patrons. Many people were scared of Catholics, whom they regarded essentially as tools of foreign powers such as the French king or the pope. Similarly, there was great suspicion of 'Dissenters' – members of any churches other than the Church of England. 'Dissenters' and Catholics alike, it was feared, were eating away at the social fabric of the country, and the policies of tolerance followed by the Whig party were greatly opposed by many. Many Anglican churchmen formed a party with the slogan 'Church in Danger', which spent its time campaigning against Catholics, Dissenters, deists, the principle of toleration and, essentially, everything that the Enlightenment had produced.

In 1778, parliament passed the Catholic Relief Act, which decriminalized Catholicism – to the enormous anger of a sizeable minority in the population. Indeed, two years after the act was passed, a Scottish aristocrat named Lord George Gordon led a huge mob to London, resulting in a week of riots in which Catholic churches were looted, foreign embassies burnt, prisons opened up, and 285 people killed.

However, things were not always this bad. It is easy to place too much faith in official doctrines or laws, and in the actions of fanatics, and overlook what was really happening on the ground among the majority of ordinary people. In England, not everyone was as bothered as Lord Gordon about the supposed encroachments of the evil 'papists'. And, while Henry Sacheverell had the support of the public in his anti-toleration crusade of 1709, in the years that followed there was a definite cooling of tempers. In the 1760s, for example, a man named William Payne, who made a living by informing on various criminals, spent some considerable effort in bringing prosecutions against Catholic priests, including Richard Challoner. He would pretend to be a potential convert to Catholicism in order to compile evidence against the Catholics. However, the Lord Mayor of London refused to act upon his accusations. Indeed, Lord Chief Justice Mansfield declared that Payne's evidence of the accused performing Mass was inadmissible, since it did not prove that they were Catholic priests: he would have to provide evidence of their ordination. He knew perfectly well that Payne would be unable to find such evidence and, as he intended, the prosecutions were dropped. It seems that, at this period, many people, including figures of considerable authority, were feeling that intolerant laws were outmoded

'Toleration is not the opposite of intoleration, but is the counterfeit of it. Both are despotisms. The one assumes to itself the right of withholding liberty of conscience, and the other of granting it. The one is the pope armed with fire and faggot, the other is the pope selling or granting indulgences.'

THOMAS PAINE,
THE RIGHTS OF MAN,
1791

and that there were more important things to worry about than what brand of Christianity different people favoured. The passing of the Catholic Relief Act typified the increasingly tolerant attitude of the ruling classes.

Reunion

Indeed, some went further. It may seem hopelessly optimistic to us today, but in the seventeenth century a number of attempts were made to open up dialogue

The case of Dr Sacheverell

In an age when, it seemed, heresy stalked the land, there were many contenders for the title 'most notorious sermon of the eighteenth century'. By common consent, however, the winner was *In Perils Among False Brethren*, preached by Dr Henry Sacheverell on 5 November 1709 in St Paul's Cathedral. The sermon was meant to commemorate the foiling of the Gunpowder Plot of 1605, when Guy Fawkes and a number of other Catholics attempted to blow up the Houses of Parliament. Sacheverell was a member of the 'Church in Danger' group, and for fully an hour and a half, we are told, with a vivid scarlet face and eyes bulging forth, he declaimed against the 'hypocrites, deists, Socinians and atheists' who were undermining the church. Still more dangerous in the good doctor's eyes, however, were the Whigs, then in power, who by their principles of toleration might end up giving 'Jews, Quakers, Mahometans, and anything' the same rights as Christians. The government, according to the preacher, was essentially opening the door to latter-day Guy Fawkeses and giving them as much gunpowder as they wanted.

So explosive was Sacheverell's rhetoric that he was actually impeached by the government and tried for treason. There followed one of the most high-profile trials of the age, during which Sacheverell's defence team read in court some of the writings of the deists and other heretics whom he had attacked, hoping to prove that the sermon had been entirely justified. Public opinion was firmly behind Sacheverell, between the Roman Catholic and Protestant churches with the aim of reuniting them. The godfather of this endeavour, sometimes known as 'syncretism', was a German Lutheran theologian named George Callixtus, who devoted enormous energies in the early seventeenth century to trying to find common ground between the different Churches. Like his contemporary Hugo Grotius in the Reformed Church, he believed that it should be possible to use the Apostles' Creed, and a belief in the authority of the Bible alone,

popularly perceived as a plain-speaking man who had had the guts to say what many had been thinking for years. In the event, Sacheverell was found guilty, a decision which led to rioting and a massive loss of support for the government – but his sentence was extraordinarily light, consisting only of a three-year ban on preaching. In the public eye, Sacheverell had been exonerated, and with him the principle of non-toleration which he represented.

The Gunpowder Plot Conspirators, c. 1605. At midnight on 4 November 1605, Guy Fawkes, sixth from the left, was discovered in a cellar under the House of Lords with 36 barrels of gunpowder and a guilty expression.

as a basis for agreement among Christians. Callixtus had profitable discussions with Calvinists, but the Catholics were less receptive. The Conference of Thorn, called by Vladislav IV of Poland in 1645, attempted to put these ideas into practice, but after several weeks of discussions the Catholic, Lutheran and Calvinist theologians who attended were unable to produce anything constructive. Sadly, Callixtus's efforts met with the greatest opposition from his fellow Lutherans, and he spent most of his life in controversy with them – ironically, his attempts to create unity had simply resulted in more division.

These attempts were not confined to those of a more liberal theological persuasion. Richard Baxter, for example, a pastor in Kidderminster, was an eminent Puritan divine in the seventeenth century. He was rather ambiguous as a churchman, being essentially Anglican but rejecting the principle of apostolic succession and turning down the post of bishop of Hereford because he did not believe in bishops. He claimed to subscribe wholly to the Canons of Dort, the classical statement of Calvinism, but did not believe in the doctrines of limited atonement (the notion that Christ's death can benefit only the elect) or double predestination. Baxter's religion revolved around the conversion, repentance and faith of the individual, which he believed was more important than toeing a particular church's party line. To this end he wrote a number of works which aimed to reconcile the doctrines of the different churches, with the ultimate aim of reuniting them. But he had no more success than Callixtus.

Nevertheless, as the seventeenth century drew to a close, the ideals which Callixtus and Baxter pioneered were becoming increasingly fashionable among Catholics too. In the 1680s, even as the French government was cruelly persecuting Protestants, there was a spirit of friendly cooperation developing among intellectuals and aristocrats who hoped to overcome the bitter divisions of nearly two centuries. John Frederick, prince of Hanover, for example, had converted from Lutheranism to

'For my part, Sir, I think all Christians, whether Papists or Protestants, agree in the essential articles, and that their differences are trivial, and rather political than religious.'

SAMUEL JOHNSON, QUOTED IN JAMES BOSWELL'S *LIFE OF JOHNSON*

Catholicism and hoped to persuade his subjects to do the same thing – but he made no attempt to force them to do so. On the contrary, he retained a healthy respect for leading Protestant thinkers, and even engaged one of them, Leibniz, as his librarian.

Leibniz, for his part, was also extremely interested in the prospect of reunion. In 1683 he wrote – though never published – a remarkable document known as the *System of Theology*, in which he provides an extraordinarily positive assessment of the doctrines and practices of the Roman Catholic Church. Indeed, it seems that there is no element of Catholicism, apart from the veneration of the Virgin Mary, that Leibniz cannot accept.

Meanwhile, on the Catholic side, Jacques Bossuet, the famous Bishop of Meux, was keen to win the Protestants back to the fold, through reasonable persuasion rather than force. Although he approved of the Revocation of the Edict of Nantes in 1685, he was never happy about the attempts to convert Huguenots by force that accompanied it. His own approach was set out in his *Exposition of Catholic Doctrine*, which was intended for a Protestant readership, and which proved extremely popular.

Between 1683 and 1700, Bossuet and Leibniz corresponded on the prospects of reunion. Unfortunately, they did not make the progress one might expect from two such enlightened minds. Although Bossuet rejected the notion of the infallibility of the pope, he did firmly believe in the infallibility of the church – by which he meant the Roman Catholic Church. Therefore, any discussion of reunion must begin with an acceptance on all sides of the falsity of Protestantism and the authority of the Council of Trent. Leibniz felt that this was an unreasonable demand, and the discussions fell flat. It didn't help that Leibniz was involved in delicate diplomatic negotiations to ensure that his employer, the Elector of Hanover, would succeed to the Crown of England – and since it was illegal for a Catholic to do that, any hint of sympathy with Rome might be politically unwise.

God in the kitchen

One of the most striking examples of common piety in the Age of Reason was an obscure, uneducated Frenchman of the late seventeenth century. Nicolas Herman, a manservant from Lorraine, tried to live his life around what he called 'the practice of the presence of God'. He was not a very good manservant, having a pronounced limp from his army days and being appallingly clumsy; but he performed his duties diligently until 1651, when, at the age of 40, he went to Paris and became a Carmelite monk. Lawrence of the Resurrection, as he was henceforth known, was put to work in the monastery's kitchen – a task he hated, but which he did anyway because it was God's will. To the surprise of the other monks, he not only did his work calmly and methodically, but spoke to God the entire time. Brother Lawrence declared that, to him, there was no difference between the time for work and the time for prayer: wherever he was, and whatever he was doing, he tried to perceive the presence of God. As he wrote to one of his friends:

There is not in the world a kind of life more sweet and delightful, than that of a continual conversation with God: the only ones who can understand it are those who practise and experience it.

Despite the friendly atmosphere of the courts of Europe and the Republic of Letters, attempts like these at reunion were doomed from the start. They were little more than the utopian dreams of elitist intellectuals. At the grassroots level, certainly on the Protestant side, there was no chance of reunion with Catholicism – because people recognized that such reunion would be less like a marriage and more like being swallowed up by Rome. Given Bossuet's arguments to Leibniz, such a fear was not unreasonable.

The age of faith

It is easy, looking at the Age of Reason, to suppose that theology was increasingly being subsumed into philosophy, and that the heartfelt faith of the Middle Ages and the

But I do not advise you to do it from that motive. It is not pleasure which we ought to seek in this exercise, but let us do it from a principle of love, and because God would have us. If I were a preacher, I would, above all other things, preach the practice of the presence of God. And if I were a spiritual director, I would advise all the world to do it. That is how necessary I think it is – and how easy, too.

FIFTH LETTER

Brother Lawrence became a minor celebrity among the hierarchy of the French Catholic Church, and he was visited by more than one archbishop, anxious to see if the reports of his humility and holiness were true. Lawrence's *Sixteen Letters* and *Spiritual Maxims* testify to his devout belief in God's presence in all things and his trust in God to see him through all things. They also testify to the way in which holy men and women continued to devote themselves to God's will, both in and out of the monasteries, even as the intellectual revolutions of the Enlightenment were at their height.

Reformation was being inevitably replaced by rationalism. That was true in some quarters, as we shall see; but in fact, the seventeenth and eighteenth centuries had their share of saints, as well as of heretics, as much as any age; and there were some important movements that recalled the faithful to a living and wholehearted religion. As the theologians bickered, the ordinary Christians were getting on with things, as they always had.

One movement of major importance to the Catholic Church was the devotion to the Sacred Heart of Jesus. This devotion involved adoration of and dedication to the physical heart of Jesus which was pierced on the cross, and which represents his love for and salvation of his people. While this devotion was fairly widespread in the Middle Ages, it received no official endorsement from the

Catholic Church. In the late seventeenth century, however, the cult acquired a new popularity, largely through the efforts of two people: John Eudes and Sister Margaret Mary Alacoque, both of whom would be canonized in the 1920s. Eudes was a priest and spiritual director from Normandy, who wrote a series of simple but profound

The Sacred Heart of Christ from the Boarding School Chapel, 1766. By Giuseppe Varotti, (1715–80), Collegio Cicognini, Prato, Tuscany, Italy.

books recommending a number of spiritual exercises which were intended to help people live the life of Christ in their own lives. He expressed this through the symbolism of the two Sacred Hearts – that of Jesus, which is the source of the believer's sanctity, and that of Mary, which is its model.

Sister Mary was an entirely different character: in contrast to the placid and scholarly Father Eudes, she was an extremely passionate woman, fiercely devoted to a religious life, who by the age of four had spent hours contemplating the sacrament and had dedicated herself to chastity. In 1674 and 1675, as a nun in Paray-le-Monial, she experienced a series of visions and revelations centred on the Sacred Heart of Jesus. She devoted herself utterly to the Sacred Heart for the rest of her life, despite the opposition of many in her order, who believed her to be emotionally unbalanced. There was certainly an element of excess in some of her devotions, which extended to writing vows to Jesus in her own blood and carving his name on her breast, but the simple virtues she embodied eventually won around the sceptics. In 1688 her convent built a chapel to the Sacred Heart, and the cult spread throughout France and elsewhere. In 1856 the festival of the Sacred Heart was extended throughout the Catholic Church; and when the French were moved to rededicate their nation to the protection of God following their defeat to Prussia in 1871, they did so by building the magnificent church of the Sacre-Coeur on Montmartre.

In Germany, meanwhile, a very different movement was taking shape. Pietism developed slowly, but its godfather was a Lutheran pastor named Johann Arndt, who lived in the early seventeenth century. Arndt was interested in how salvation is won by Christ, but instead of stressing the objectivity of this salvation (although he did not deny it) he preferred to focus on its effect on the individual believer. Specifically, he thought that this should take an ethical form, based on a new relationship with the risen Saviour, in which the believer lives the life

'If you are in an abyss of dryness and weakness, go and bury yourself in the loving Heart of Jesus. If you are in an abyss of poverty and stripped of all things, go to the Heart of Jesus. He will enrich you. If you find yourself so weak that you fall at every step, go and bury yourself in the strength of his Sacred Heart. He will deliver you.'

MARGARET MARY ALACOQUE, *THE SACRED HEART OF JESUS, AN ABYSS OF WISDOM AND LOVE* of Christ. This, not dogmatics or loyalty to a particular church, is what is important. A century later, ideas like these coalesced in the work of Philip Spener, whose *Pious Wishes* of 1675 gave the movement its name. Spener shared Arndt's distaste for traditional doctrinal disputes and ecclesiastical party loyalties, and his wish to make Christianity a matter of living correctly. Without that, and

A methodical preacher

If you liked sermons, 1739 was a great year to be in England. In February, George Whitefield, an Anglican just returned from America and about to make his reputation as one of the greatest preachers of all time, delivered his first open-air diatribe in Bristol. Two hundred people listened to him. The next time, there were 2,000. Soon there were 20,000. Elated by his success, Whitefield invited his friend John Wesley to come to the city and try it for himself.

Wesley had had a chequered career. Born in 1703 to Puritan parents, he had grown up with a severe religion which stressed the necessity of holy living. His attempts to live up to this ideal had not always made him popular. Taking up a ministerial post in America, he had alienated his congregation and left under a cloud. In 1738, however, as he was attending a Bible-reading in Oxford, Wesley had a change of heart. As he listened to Paul's letter to the Romans, he realized that true Christianity was not about *doing* anything, however holy it might seem. It was about knowing Christ personally. If you had that, a holy life would follow naturally.

This was the message that Wesley began preaching to the crowds in 1739, and he continued to preach it for the next 50 years. Where Whitefield's sermons were stunning displays of impassioned rhetoric, Wesley's aimed to persuade the hearers' reason rather than sway their emotion. All the same, Wesley's sermons were generally punctuated by shrieks and wails, as people collapsed in convulsive fits, only to be calmed again by the flow of words from the small, neatly dressed figure with the golden mouth and hypnotic gaze.

Wesley was deeply influenced by German Pietism, and indeed spent some time with the Moravian community at Herrnhut, one of Pietism's most important strongholds. But he lacked the suspicion that most Pietists had for doctrinal orthodoxy, and his message touched hundreds of thousands. It was a message of warmth and salvation, of the need for cooperation between a gracious God and a responsive humanity – for Wesley was, theologically, an Arminian, something the knowledge of God from the Holy Spirit, you can have only a false Christianity.

Inevitably, these pious ideas resulted in conflict – this time with the orthodox Lutheran theologians who interpreted them as an attack on traditional doctrine and practice. The Pietists attacked back. The radical Pietist Gottfried Arnold declared that the history of Christianity

stricter Whitefield was not happy about at all. Wesley spent most of his life travelling Britain by horseback – often over 60 miles (100 km) a day – and delivered four or five sermons a day, beginning at 5.00 a.m. sharp. His work and that of his colleagues gave rise to a new movement, almost a church within the Church of England. Their opponents dubbed them 'Methodists' for their ethical rigour – a good name in Wesley's case, who remained something of an obsessive compulsive all his life, keeping journals in which he carefully noted each day's temptations and the degree to which he resisted them. His followers were regarded with suspicion by the authorities, who feared them as a source of dissension led by a dangerous rabble-rouser. After Wesley's death in 1791, the Methodists did separate from the Church of England, becoming an important church which today has 70 million members worldwide.

Portrait of John Wesley by Nathaniel Hope, 1766.

was the history of a war between mystics and hidebound authorities, and made it quite clear whose side he was on. The most notorious Pietist, however, was undoubtedly Johann Dippel, who was born – appropriately, given his stormy career – at the Frankenstein castle near Darmstadt in 1673. Indeed, Dippel was an alchemist and medical experimenter, who claimed to have discovered the 'Philosopher's Stone' but subsequently lost it, and who is said to have inspired Mary Shelley's 'Frankenstein' story by experimenting on corpses from the local graveyard. He is supposed to have died gruesomely, too – his corpse was discovered in an agonized position in his study, bright blue in colour: Dippel, we are told, had discovered the dye Prussian Blue, but unwisely drank it and poisoned himself.

Dippel believed that the established churches were essentially the enemy of true Christianity, which was about ethics, not dogma. His outspoken attacks on every 'sect' he could think of – from Lutheranism to Wolffianism – led to his being imprisoned and exiled with monotonous regularity. In 1729 he produced his notorious *True Evangelical Demonstration*, in which he attacked the traditional belief that Christ died in the place of sinners. Rather, Christ's death should be interpreted as God curing humanity like a doctor, inspiring us to lead better lives. The book was one of the most controversial of the eighteenth century, and for generations Dippel's name would, in Germany, become proverbial shorthand for irrationality and enthusiasm.

A more moderate kind of spiritual renewal was on offer in the English-speaking world. It had been kicked off, in part, by William Law, whose *A Serious Call to a Devout and Holy Life* was published to great acclaim in 1728. Like the Pietists, Law believed that Christianity was a matter of living correctly, and he was shocked by the lifestyles of many people he met. While professing Christianity, they did not seem to be living it. His *Serious Call* is full of entertaining vignettes of fictional characters whom Law uses to illustrate his point – but his tone is wholly different from Dippel's. Law believed firmly in the reasonableness of Christianity and believed, moreover, that a reasonable presentation of its ethical demands would have powerful persuasive effects. In this he seems to have been quite right, as his book made a great impression on many, including John Wesley and Samuel Johnson.

In his later years, Law became interested in the mystical theology of the medieval heterodox writer Jacob Boehme. His works from this time emphasize the natural likeness of the human soul to God, to whom it is naturally impelled. Through the indwelling of Christ in the soul, God is to be found within, through a radical rejection of the outside world and its values. Law's spirituality was thus a dualist one, driven by a fundamental division between the values of the world and the values of God, and focusing on the role of the human free will in turning from the one to the other.

These ideas had much in common with those of the Quakers, who had been founded in England in 1647 by George Fox. Fox believed that religion was not about dogma or church membership: rather, it was about the individual's personal relationship with Christ. His followers therefore rejected all ecclesiastical structure, including priests and sacraments, because these contradicted the principle of the individual's direct access to God through Christ. For this, many were persecuted, tortured or executed by the English authorities in the latter half of the seventeenth century. Many fled to America, where they were subjected to similar attacks by the Puritans. Their official name was the 'Society of Friends', but as time went by they placed more and more emphasis on the inward relation of the believer to Christ, to such an extent that their services consisted of everyone sitting in silence. The term 'Quaker' came about as a derogatory description of this. Yet the Quakers bore ridicule and persecution with exemplary grace. When the

'One cannot imagine anything more absurd than wise, sublime and heavenly prayers, tagged onto a foolish worthless life where neither work nor leisure, time nor money, are under the direction of those same wise and heavenly prayers.'

WILLIAM LAW,
A SERIOUS CALL TO A DEVOUT AND HOLY LIFE CHAPTER 1

Quaker William Penn founded Pennsylvania in 1682, he set out a constitution which was a model of tolerance and freedom, ensuring religious freedom for all its inhabitants – which was more than the Puritans had ever done.

The New Philosophy

The Age of Reason was not only a time of scientific discovery and religious controversy. A consequence and a cause of both of these things was the revolution in philosophy that was going on at the same time. To the Enlightenment mind, there was no clear-cut difference between what we would call philosophy and science. Both activities were known by both names, and their practitioners were 'philosophers' – the word 'scientist' had not yet been invented. Thus, the new movements in philosophy had a direct bearing on science and on religious thought, more so than they might today.

Another important factor in the influence of philosophy at this time was the fact that it was literally a popular movement. Philosophy had been taught in universities for centuries, but it was an 'official' kind of philosophy that had been formulated in the Middle Ages and revolved around certain set ideas, issues and jargon. One of the reasons that the 'New Philosophy' was so controversial was that its practitioners consciously sought to ignore or even replace this traditional 'scholastic' philosophy. Indeed, they were not even university professors, but rank amateurs – Descartes was a soldier, and Locke a doctor. To some, these unprofessional meddlers hardly merited the title 'philosopher' at all. Yet it was they who would mould the thought of the Enlightenment.

Descartes

Perhaps more than any other, the man who famously declared, 'I think, therefore I am', was responsible for the passing of the old world of the Renaissance and the ushering in of the Age of Reason.

René Descartes was born in 1596 at La Hayes, in France (the town has since been renamed simply 'Descartes'). He was educated at the famous Jesuit college of La Fléche, and then embarked on a life of adventure, travelling around Europe and enlisting with various armies fighting the Thirty Years War. In 1619 he became convinced that his mission was to found a new philosophy, one that would sweep away the remnants of medieval scholasticism, and he gave up his military career. Having the good fortune to come from an old and monied family, however, he had no need to get any other job, and he continued to travel around Europe, ending up in Holland.

Portrait of René Descartes by Frans Hals.

Fireside philosophy

Descartes' philosophical epiphany came to him in 1619 while
sitting, he tells us, in a 'stove' – which is a tempting image,
although he presumably means a room heated by a stove.
The ideas that he first pondered then are elaborated in his
Meditations, published over 20 years later, which contain by
far the most well-known elements of his philosophy.

Descartes' aim in the *Meditations* is to establish some
certainty, and to do so through reason, not by appealing to
external authority. He points out that our senses often lead us
astray; indeed, it is possible that everything that seems real is
merely a dream, or a hallucination caused by a malicious demon.
There was nothing new about this kind of epistemological
scepticism, which went back to ancient Greek thought, but
Descartes hoped to use it constructively, by test-driving all his
beliefs to destruction. If he doubted everything as radically as
possible, but then found some belief that he could not doubt,
then he could take that to be certain. And Descartes did find
one such belief. However much one doubts, there is one thing
that cannot seriously be doubted – one's own existence. If I am
doubting, then there must be a *me* to do the doubting. The
point is summarized (in the Latin translation of the *Discourse*)
in Descartes' famous pronouncement, *Cogito ergo sum* –
I think, therefore I am.

Having established this, Descartes then hopes to show that
the physical world really does exist as it appears to; but he takes
what might seem the rather roundabout route of first proving
that God exists. He does this by some rather shifty reasoning,
appealing to the fact that he has an idea of God, the perfect
being; but this idea could have come only from a really perfect
being. Therefore, God exists. Since God is good, he wouldn't let
Descartes believe that there is a physical world if it weren't so.
So the world does exist after all, and life can go on.

'Good sense is, of all things among men, the most well distributed – for everyone thinks he has so much of it, that even those who are hard to satisfy in other things don't generally want any more of it than they already have.'

RENÉ DESCARTES,
DISCOURSE ON METHOD CHAPTER 1

'It is not enough to have a good mind. The main thing is to use it well.'

RENÉ DESCARTES,
DISCOURSE ON METHOD CHAPTER 1

The fact that a Catholic chose to live in this stronghold of the Reformed faith is itself a clue to the undogmatic, free-thinking nature of Descartes' philosophy.

In 1637 Descartes published a selection of scientific essays, prefaced by his famous *Discourse on Method*, which set out his philosophical principles. This, together with his *Meditations on First Philosophy* of 1641, made him famous, and Descartes began to correspond with some of the greatest minds of his day. Some, such as the Catholic Jansenist theologian Antoine Arnauld, engaged him in critical philosophical discussion; others, such as the Reformed theologian Gisbert Voetius, denounced his philosophy as new-fangled nonsense and impiety. 'Cartesianism' became a highly controversial movement, alternately embraced and condemned in universities and pulpits throughout Europe.

Descartes' thought revolved around a basic belief that the world was essentially comprehensible, and that the key to understanding it lay in thinking carefully. He believed that if one understood something clearly and distinctly, one could be sure that it was true. Indeed, he believed that some ideas were intrinsically 'clear and distinct', and that this was the mark of truth. He was greatly influenced by mathematics, a field in which he excelled – inventing modern coordinate geometry, which is why we talk of 'Cartesian' coordinates. In maths, the fact that $2+2=4$ is obvious and undeniable if you only consider it calmly and coolly, and Descartes hoped to apply the same method to philosophy and science. He declared that whenever we fall into error, this is not because of any defect in our understanding. On the contrary, human understanding is, in itself, infallible. Mistakes arise when we choose to believe something without properly submitting it to the understanding. And that is a matter of the will, not the understanding.

It should be clear that this twin notion of the comprehensibility of the natural world, and the ability of the unaided human reason to understand it without too much difficulty provided some care is taken, was a revolution to those brought up in the intellectual traditions of the Renaissance. Think of the world of Paracelsus, where an organic universe is known only through esoteric secrets and mysteries, preserved in magical tongues, and where occult forces may be manipulated to heal the sick, predict the future, or create gold. The gulf between this outlook, and the rationalism of Descartes, is surely greater than that between any other two thinkers who lived only a century apart.

In 1649, Queen Christina of Sweden invited the famous philosopher to her court. Descartes was not happy in Sweden, partly because the Queen had him engaged in unsuitable activities such as writing a comic play, but mainly because she insisted on being taught philosophy at 5.00 a.m. Descartes, who was notoriously lazy, was used to staying in bed until 11.00 a.m.; and the shock of the early mornings killed him within six months.

His philosophy, however, lived on. Cartesianism was one of the hot issues of the second half of the seventeenth century, and Descartes' ideas were soon being defended and developed by subsequent thinkers.

Cartesianism and beyond

Some hoped to use Descartes' philosophy to express Christian faith, creating a Cartesian theology rather like the scholastic Aristotelian theology they wanted to replace. For example, Antoine Arnauld believed that Cartesianism offered the best basis for a Christian philosophy, since it proved doctrines such as the existence of God and the immortality of the soul. He saw many correspondences between Descartes' philosophy and that of Augustine. At the same time, the followers of the Reformed 'Remonstrant' theologian, Johannes Cocceius, tried to combine his theology with the philosophy of Descartes. It is not clear exactly why they did this, other than that they recognized the value in reinforcing their theology with a substantial metaphysical system, and had

What's the big idea?

One concept in Enlightenment philosophy looms large over all the others – the 'idea'. Some philosophers seem to talk about nothing else. What do they all mean by this innocuous word? An 'idea' is practically anything to be found in the mind, and the imprecision with which it is defined was one of the causes of philosophical disagreement. It could be a mental *image* – what is produced mentally if you imagine something. Or it could be a *definition* of something, a concept. Descartes, at least, understood the difference here and explained it well – if we think of a chiliagon (a shape with a thousand sides) there is no way we can form a mental image of this, but we can certainly form a conception of it – we understand what it means.

Finally, an 'idea' could be a *perception*. Philosophers believed that when you look at, say, a table, the square brown thing in your field of perception – the thing that you *actually*, *directly perceive* – was not the table itself but simply an 'idea' that was produced by the effect of light reflecting off the real table and hitting your eyes. In modern philosophy, 'ideas' in this sense are known as 'sense-data', and there has been much

a desire to do so in a modern way. To more traditional thinkers, however, such as the theologian Gisbert Voetius, Descartes and Cocceius were part and parcel of pernicious modern free thinking, fit only to be condemned in the same breath.

Arnold Geulincx, a Dutch philosopher, formulated a philosophy based on that of Descartes but with far more of a role for God. Descartes had drawn a clear line between mind and matter, two separate realms with nothing in common, but Geulincx focused on the Divine Mind, which underlies and controls the world of matter. Indeed, every event is directly caused by God. When we play snooker, it looks as if one ball strikes another and causes it (hopefully) to head towards a pocket – but Geulincx suggests that it is actually God who moves the second ball.

discussion since the eighteenth century over whether they exist at all – that is, whether it makes sense to distinguish at all between the immediate object of perception and the object itself.

All of this led to considerable confusion. When a philosopher spoke of 'the idea of a table', he might mean practically anything, from his immediate perception of *this* table, to his memory of it, to his understanding of what the word 'table' meant. Today, scholars are divided over precisely what the various philosophers meant, a confusion that was shared by the philosophers themselves. For example, Malebranche, who was perhaps the most committed to the 'sense-data' theory, conducted a long correspondence with Arnauld about it throughout the 1680s and 90s, in which the substantial disagreement between the two (Arnauld believed that physical objects are perceived directly) was muddled by their disagreement over what it was, precisely, that they disagreed about.

This is known as 'occasionalism', and its most famous proponent was Nicolas Malebranche, a French priest who enjoyed a very high reputation as a philosopher in the generation after Descartes. Malebranche believed that God is so closely united to his creation that we can think of him as the 'place' in which minds exist, just as space is the place in which physical objects are located. Every sensation that we have is given to us directly by God, and every time we act on the world it is God who actually does it. Here, then, we find Cartesianism wedded to Catholic theology, although Malebranche did come under fire for his understanding of the relation between God and humanity, and in 1709, six years before his death, his principal work *The Search for Truth* was placed on the Index of books forbidden by the Catholic Church.

Malebranche is often considered one of the leading proponents of a 'school' of thought known as 'rationalism', which means not a general faith in reason (which was becoming the defining feature of the Enlightenment) but a particular philosophical position regarding *how* reason understands the world. Descartes himself is often thought of as the founder of modern philosophical rationalism, and indeed its basic principle was very close to his heart: the twin idea that the world is intrinsically comprehensible, and that it is mirrored, in some way, by thought. In other

The Dutch philosopher Baruch de Spinoza. Crayon engraving by Jean Charles Francois, 1762.

words, it is possible to determine what is true by careful study of concepts. The philosopher who embodied these principles par excellence was Baruch de Spinoza.

Spinoza was an inoffensive man who led a quiet and blameless existence, and who was universally loathed during his lifetime and for decades afterwards. Born in 1632 in the Netherlands, the son of an orthodox Jewish merchant of Spanish background, Spinoza rebelled against the life of a rabbi for which he was marked. His sister tried to prevent his inheriting any of his father's estate; Spinoza therefore took her to court, won his inheritance, and then renounced it all. He was expelled and excommunicated by the Jewish community of Amsterdam for what they regarded as his heresy, and is even said to have been attacked by an assassin; but he continued to live quietly in the Netherlands, teaching philosophy and supporting himself on very modest means by grinding lenses. He turned down the offer to write a book dedicated to Louis XIV of France in exchange for a handsome pension; he also turned down the offer of a professorship at the University of Heidelberg. He did not feel that such official sponsorship of his work was compatible with the peace and freedom he needed, and he retained this peace and freedom until his death in 1677 from consumption, exacerbated by the glass dust to which his profession exposed him.

'Every idea in us which is absolute, or adequate and perfect, is true.'

BARUCH DE SPINOZA,
ETHICS II, PROP. 34

Spinoza's philosophy was constructed from very similar premises to that of Descartes, a man he greatly admired. But where Descartes separated the mental world from the material world, Spinoza believed that they were two sides of the same coin. There is only one substance, or thing that exists in its own right; and Spinoza identifies this substance as God. And every object in the world is simply a 'mode' of God. But the one substance can be understood as existing under two different 'attributes' – thought and extension, or the mental world and the physical one. It is as if we could view the world through two pairs of tinted spectacles – the same objects are perceived each time, but they appear different. Thus,

Spinoza overcomes the vexed Cartesian problem of how the mind interacts with the body by simply asserting that the mind is the body, understood under the attribute of thought rather than extension.

To Spinoza's contemporaries, all this was atheism, because Spinoza recognized no God apart from the physical world. It would have been more accurate, of course, to say that Spinoza recognized the physical world only as existing within God. His conception of the one reality existing in two 'attributes' meant that, for Spinoza, the world of thought was an exact mirror of the physical world – for they were really the same world. So a mental conception of reality – an idea – is actually the same thing as the object it is an idea of. This meant that an idea could be guaranteed to be true and accurate provided it was clear enough. Spinoza's equivalent to Descartes' 'clear and distinct idea' is the 'adequate idea', an idea that has an *intrinsic* mark of truth; and he is confident that if we confine ourselves to what we understand adequately we can construct a perfect account of reality.

Spinoza did this himself in his masterpiece, the *Ethics*. The work is set out like a geometry textbook, made up of definitions and propositions, which are formally proved on the basis of the definitions and earlier propositions. Spinoza's aim is to begin with clear and evident definitions, and then work up to a detailed account of human existence. Thus, the first definition is the dry 'By "cause of itself" I understand that whose essence involves existence; or, that whose nature cannot be conceived except as existing.' He then proves the existence and nature of God and the mind before moving on to how human beings can and should live, coolly dissecting every human thought and emotion, before proving the final proposition of the book: 'Blessedness is not the reward of virtue, but virtue itself: nor do we enjoy it because we constrain our lusts, but, on the contrary, because we enjoy it we can constrain our lusts.'

Not only was Spinoza's universe a pantheistic and

geometrical one, it was also one ruled by necessity and fate. This was the other main reason he was disliked by contemporary philosophers – the fact that he believed that everything that exists and occurs does so necessarily. How, then, can people be free? For Spinoza, freedom is a matter of self-determination. The more the mind frees itself of passion, the more it is active and able to consider things from the point of view of eternity; and the more it does this, the more like God it is.

Other philosophies

If rationalism was one way of developing the heritage of Descartes, another was known as 'empiricism'. The notion that there were these two rival schools of thought, rationalism and empiricism, in the seventeenth and eighteenth centuries, and that every philosopher belonged to one or the other, is the traditional way of thinking of this period of philosophy, and indeed goes back to Thomas Reid, an eighteenth-century representative of empiricism. It is simplistic, but helpful in understanding the basic differences between thinkers of this time.

Where rationalists believed that all secure knowledge is based on innate ideas, ideas that are part and parcel of the mind, and on studying the nature of these ideas, empiricists did not believe in innate ideas at all. They believed that all knowledge comes from experience, and that we learn about the world by testing our ideas against it. And where rationalism held sway on the continent, empiricism was the dominant philosophy in Britain.

The empiricists drew much of their inspiration from Thomas Hobbes, a man renowned for his cynical account of human life, which he famously described as naturally 'solitary, poor, nasty, brutish and short' – although his own life was entirely happy and lasted 91 years. Like his younger contemporary Descartes, Hobbes believed that the truth could be had provided we reason clearly enough, but he also thought that all the ideas we reason about come from experience.

'Insofar as the mind understands all things as necessary it has more power over the emotions.'

BARUCH DE SPINOZA,
ETHICS V, PROP. 6

This insight was powerfully developed by John Locke. In his mammoth *Essay Concerning Human Understanding*, published in 1690, Locke sought to set out a comprehensive empiricism. All ideas come from experience – either directly from sensation, or from reflection, the process of creating new ideas from ones we already have. Learning, for Locke, is rather like putting together a jigsaw puzzle, except that the pieces are our ideas, and we can know that we have put it together correctly only by comparing it to the real world (the picture on the box, if you like).

The only problem, which Locke himself was well aware of, was that if all knowledge and understanding revolves around the manipulation of these 'ideas', and we never actually experience the real world directly, then we can't know anything for sure about the real world. If all we ever see is the jigsaw pieces, then we can never really compare them to the picture on the box. However, Locke was nothing if not reasonable, and he believed that while certainty of the kind that Descartes sought was elusive, at least in matters of physics and epistemology, we can still have reasonable probability. After all, he admonished the sceptic who feared that the world might not really exist, try putting your hand in a glass furnace and see if your philosophical doubts are still as strong.

Locke's common-sense way of doing philosophy was extremely influential, and British philosophy is still imbued with his spirit. In particular, the respect – almost deference – that many French thinkers had for English philosophy and science meant that the eighteenth century saw Locke-style empiricism competing for space with Cartesianism and its descendants in France.

But the Lockean philosophy came under attack from a variety of directions. One of his earliest opponents – although Locke himself seems to have considered his objections not worth responding to – was Leibniz. He is usually considered one of the rationalist philosophers, but his epistemology was more subtle than that of Malebranche or Spinoza. Like them, he believed in innate

ideas, because he recognized that a thoroughgoing
empiricism like Locke's can never result in true
knowledge. If Locke were right, and all knowledge comes
from experience alone, then all we would ever have would
be, say, *this* particular experience and *that* particular
experience. We would be unable to extrapolate from these
particular experiences and understand the general rules
by which the world is governed. Indeed, as we shall see
in Chapter 9, it would be by accepting this unpalatable
consequence of thoroughgoing empiricism that David
Hume, decades later, would take the tradition to extremes.

Leibniz, then, believed in innate ideas, but argued that
it was still necessary for experience to coax them out. In
place of the 'white paper' of Locke, Leibniz compares the
mind to a block of marble with lines inside it marking out
the form of a statue. The block contains the form within
it, but it is necessary to chip away at it to reveal the
statue.

Nevertheless, Leibniz is ultimately compelled to
uphold the innateness of all ideas, because of his
notoriously peculiar metaphysical system. The most
famous element of his philosophy is the concept of
'monads', a system which Leibniz developed in his later
years, and whose truth he claimed to demonstrate by pure
reason alone.

Monads are immaterial substances, infinite in
number, which underlie the physical world which we
perceive. Indeed, each monad itself perceives the world –
although Leibniz does not mean 'perceive' necessarily to
involve consciousness – and each monad has a unique
perspective on the world. In fact, the physical world
simply *is* the perceptions of all the monads – for monads
alone are true substances, really existing in themselves.
We could think of each monad as a tiny film projector,
showing a film of the world from its own point of view –
except that there are an infinite number of them, each
projecting a slightly different view of the same scene.
And each monad perceives some parts of the world more

clearly than others, and is intimately connected to the part that it perceives most clearly. Every part of the world, no matter how small, has its own controlling monad, and there is a sort of hierarchy of monads, because every part

of every part of the world has its own monad, and so on for ever. We ourselves are monads, for the human soul is nothing other than a monad that perceives a human body perfectly, and which furthermore has consciousness too.

Leibniz with Sophie Charlotte, the Electress of Brandenburg. It was at sophisticated courts such as this one that Leibniz and those like him hoped to spread the Enlightenment message of reason and progress. Engraving, 1855, from a drawing by Theobald Freiherr von Oer (1807–85).

'There is a perfect harmony between the perceptions of the monad and the motions of the bodies, pre-established at the outset... Herein consists the concord and physical union of the soul and the body, which exists without the one being able to change the laws of the other.'

GOTTFRIED LEIBNIZ,
*PRINCIPLES OF
NATURE AND OF
GRACE*

All that monads ever do is perceive – they are perfectly simple substances, which means that they have no parts, and therefore no way of acting on each other or changing each other. It is remarkable, therefore, that their perceptions all 'match' – that is, that the film shown by one projector is of the same scene as that shown by its neighbour, albeit from a slightly different perspective. Indeed, each monad exists in its own, totally solipsistic universe, eternally dreaming its own dream, never coming into contact with its neighbours. The fact that everything 'matches', according to Leibniz, is an excellent proof of the existence of God, who ensures that there is perfect harmony in all things. In creating the monads and their perceptions – when deciding what film they would all be watching – God chose from a variety of possibilities, but being perfectly good he naturally chose the best possible one.

Before he published these rather startling ideas, Leibniz wrote about them to Arnauld. Arnauld pointed out that these metaphysics had worrying implications for free will – if the universe operates according to a divinely pre-established harmony, selected from among others to maximize the amount of goodness in the world, then does this mean that everything is necessary, even the will of God? Is Leibniz's philosophy any different from Spinoza's, apart from the minor difference of featuring an infinity of bizarre substances rather than a single one? Leibniz protested that it was quite different, but unlike most people he respected Spinoza and even met him once to discuss philosophy, and he was well aware what a dangerous line he was treading.

The wonderfully baroque metaphysics of Leibniz represents the pinnacle of Enlightenment rationalist philosophy. But it seems a long way from the world of common sense, and it was a philosophy that matched common sense that the English-speaking philosophers hoped to create. Foremost among those who inherited the tradition of Lockean empiricism in the eighteenth century were the Scottish philosopher Thomas Reid and the Irish cleric George Berkeley. Reid rejected the distinction – maintained by Locke as by Descartes – between objects and ideas. He picked up on the problem with Locke's theories mentioned earlier. Locke claims that all we directly perceive are ideas, which are caused by external objects – but if that's so, then how does Locke know anything about these external objects? Reid has little time for Locke's protestations that we can't have certainty about them but there is still probability. How can he know even that? Reid therefore argues that there are no 'ideas' at all, in the sense of mental images that are the direct objects of perception. Rather, we perceive external objects directly, an opinion far more in line with common sense, although not without its own difficulties.

Berkeley – who became bishop of Cloyne, and who gave his name to the famous American university, although he pronounced it 'Barcley' – is famous for taking the opposite approach to Reid, and upholding Locke's belief in ideas while rejecting external objects. He managed this because he was a more thoroughgoing empiricist than Locke: if we can think about things only if we have an idea of them, and if we can have an idea of something only by experiencing it, then the notion of 'external objects distinct from perceived ideas' makes no sense at all! By definition we never experience these things, so not only can we not know about them, but we cannot even talk about them in the first place. Berkeley instead argued powerfully that our immediate perceptions are the real world. The square blob that appears in my mind when I look at the table is the table. Berkeley felt that in arguing in this way he was championing common sense, but he was much misunderstood in his day: he was thought to be denying that objects exist at all. After all, the square blob ceases to exist when I am not looking at it. So is the world just a dream? Dr Johnson famously remarked, 'I refute Berkeley thus!' while kicking a rock,

**Thomas Reid.
Engraving by
Ridley.**

*'There is no
greater
impediment to
the advancement
of knowledge
than the
ambiguity
of words.'*

THOMAS REID,
*ESSAYS ON THE
INTELLECTUAL
POWERS OF MAN*

'All the choir of heaven and furniture of the earth, in a word all those bodies which compose the mighty frame of the world, have not any subsistence without a mind.'

GEORGE BERKELEY,
*PRINCIPLES OF
HUMAN KNOWLEDGE*
PARA. 6

and on another occasion slammed a door in the face of an admirer of Berkeley, suggesting that he ought to be able to walk through it.

Berkeley is often thought to have suggested that unperceived objects do still exist because God perceives them. In fact, while he toyed with this idea, what he actually said is that they still exist in the sense that we would perceive them if we looked in that direction. Here he anticipates the later philosophical position of phenomenalism, which holds that the statement 'There is a table in the next room' actually means 'If you go into the next room you will see a table.' However, God does play a central role in the system, because in the absence of material objects to give us our ideas it is he who causes them all. Like Leibniz, Berkeley argues that the perfect regularity of phenomena is a sure sign of God's existence, power and goodness.

Faith, Reason and Authority

The one thing that rationalists and empiricists had in common was that they both believed that knowledge was accessible through the use of human faculties. In the second chapter of his *Discourse on Method*, Descartes presented four rules that he had deduced to ensure correct reasoning. He tells us the first of these:

I would not accept anything as true which I did not clearly know to be true. That is to say, I would carefully avoid being over hasty or prejudiced, and I would understand nothing by my judgments beyond what presented itself so clearly and distinctly to my mind that I had no occasion to doubt it.

Here we have the essence of rationalism, the notion that the truth of an idea can be ascertained by considering the nature of that idea. But Descartes' principle is all-encompassing: he will accept as true *nothing* that he cannot *know* to be true in this way. Done thoroughly, this results in the method of doubt that we saw in the previous chapter; and among the things that are doubted and then assessed by reason in this way are religious claims. In other words, in Descartes' world, reason is the final arbiter of what is true. We cannot take anything to be true simply on authority, whether that is the authority of the Bible, of the church or of tradition.

As we might expect, this notion is part and parcel of philosophical rationalism. If you can construct a system of metaphysics and ethics on the basis of a few self-evident postulates, as Spinoza attempted to do, then there is little place for traditional authority – and indeed, one of the things Spinoza got into trouble for was his pioneering work in biblical criticism, the attempt to understand the Bible as a product of human history rather than as a divine revelation. And what could be more inimical to the traditional authorities than Leibniz's hope that, one day, all disagreements would be resolved with little more than 'Let us calculate'?

'The universal disposition of this age is bent upon a rational religion.'

THOMAS SPRAT,
*HISTORY OF THE
ROYAL SOCIETY*, 1667

This approach was rapidly becoming dominant within intellectual circles. It was shared not only by rationalists in the philosophical sense but by empiricists too. In his *Essay Concerning Human Understanding*, Locke considers the authority of revelation as a potential source of knowledge:

Whatever God hath revealed, is certainly true; no doubt can be made of it. This is the proper object of faith. But whether it be a divine revelation, or no, reason must judge; which can never permit the mind to reject a greater evidence to embrace what is less evident, nor allow it to entertain probability in opposition to knowledge and certainty.

BOOK IV, CHAPTER 18

In other words, we can rest assured that divine revelation is true and trustworthy. But we cannot necessarily assume that what we are hearing really *is* divine revelation – and to determine that, it is necessary to look at the evidence and decide for ourselves. So while Locke pays lip service to the importance of revelation, in reality revelation, like any other source of information, must be subject to rational scrutiny.

For Locke himself, this approach was quite compatible with orthodox Christianity, and he spent considerable time not only poring over the scriptures but publishing his thoughts on them, principally in a series of paraphrases of and notes on books of the New Testament, which found a wide readership when published shortly after his death. Indeed, Locke's view of revelation represented an important element of the typically Anglican 'common

sense' approach to faith. It was an approach that rejected
the authoritarianism that was regarded as one of the chief
flaws of Roman Catholicism, and which felt that the
reliability of the scriptures, and the truth of orthodox
doctrine, would inevitably commend themselves to the
individual enquirer through their own merits.

But thinkers such as Locke were starting to push the
point in a way that some felt was going, perhaps, a little
too far. Locke did it himself in *The Reasonableness of
Christianity as Delivered in the Scriptures*, published
anonymously in 1695. In this work, to be sure, Locke
concluded that the doctrines of orthodox Christianity were
true, or at least most of them, and that the Bible is to be
trusted. But what angered many was the fact that he felt
himself qualified to issue such a judgment in the first
place. Wasn't he essentially setting up human reason as
the final arbiter of revelation? And didn't this open up the
possibility that reason might reject that revelation?

The problem

What was happening during the Enlightenment was
essentially the disruption of a unified, organic system of
thought that had developed during the Middle Ages. One
of the founding principles of that system of thought was
the essential agreement between faith and reason – a
principle tempered by the equally important one that faith
and reason are not equal partners. What reason tells us is
correct, but faith tells us more.

This notion of faith 'perfecting' reason is exemplified
in the work of Thomas Aquinas, the greatest of the
medieval scholastic philosophers. For instance, in his
magisterial *Summa Theologiae*, Aquinas argues that God's
existence is certain: indeed, there are five different ways
of proving it, through the exercise of reason alone. At
the same time, scripture and the revelation that has
been given to the church confirms that there is indeed
a God. But the information conveyed by revelation is
more extensive: it tells us that God is a Trinity, that he

*'That the Holy
Scripture is so
plain, in all
things necessary
to salvation, that
it may be rightly
understood, or
interpreted, by
any man of
sound judgment,
is a proposition,
which one would
imagine should
not be
questioned by
any Christian.'*

ROBERT GROVE,
BISHOP OF
CHICHESTER
(1691–96),
*THE PROTESTANT
AND POPISH WAY OF
INTERPRETING
SCRIPTURE,
IMPARTIALLY
COMPARED*

became incarnate in Christ, and that he saves us.

Aquinas's influence over Catholicism only increased with the Reformation, as Catholic theologians went back to his work for new inspiration against the Protestants. Funnily enough, despite his status as the pre-eminent medieval Catholic authority, Aquinas was also popular with many Protestants. Theodore Beza, the most significant

Pilgrims in the Vatican's St Peter's Square for the opening of the 15th World Youth Day, August 2000.

Reformed theologian after Calvin himself, was a particular fan. Thus, the approach to faith and reason that Aquinas represented was, by the time of the Enlightenment, deeply entrenched throughout Christendom, both Catholic and Protestant.

Together with this insistence on faith perfecting reason, the medieval thinkers and their successors developed the idea that, although all the different branches of knowledge form a coherent whole, it can still be divided into different disciplines, each of which has its own method of enquiry. For example, it would be inappropriate to use the methods of mathematicians to find out truths of morality; and it would be wrong to expect any moral findings to have the same level of certainty and accuracy as maths. This was a common-sense view that went back to Aristotle.

*'Although
arguments from
human reason
cannot prove
what must be
received on faith,
all the same,
sacred doctrine
argues from
articles of faith
to other truths.'*

THOMAS AQUINAS,
SUMMA THEOLOGIAE
I.1.8

The new philosophy was breaking this understanding of human knowledge apart. Descartes' avowed aim to transfer the methods of mathematics to metaphysics and physical science was an assault on the traditional division of the sciences, intensified by Spinoza's choice to present his ethics in a form such as that of a geometry textbook. Yet even more radical than this new approach – which was shocking enough to old-fashioned philosophy professors – was the abandoning of the old understanding of faith and reason that it entailed. If Descartes and Spinoza could really deduce the most subtle doctrines of divine and human nature through the power of mathematics alone, then clearly there was not much need for revelation.

As the new philosophy confronted the old, and gave way in its turn to a variety of new and often radically opposed methodologies, the issue of faith and reason was up for grabs, and a bewildering variety of possibilities became available.

Reason supporting faith

One option was, as far as possible, to hang on to the old way of seeing things. Many found this surprisingly easy throughout the period, and it is a useful reminder of the fact that the Enlightenment was not a matter of a new way of thinking simply replacing the old, but of new ways of thinking jostling for space with the old.

Thus, many saw new knowledge and sciences as opportunities for bolstering traditional faith. One interesting example of this was the emerging science of chronology. One of the leading scholars of the first half of the seventeenth century was a French Catholic theologian named Denis Petau. Following the fashion of the time, Petau Latinized his name to become the far more impressive-sounding Dionysius Petavius, and he was a man of considerable and wide-ranging talents – not just a theologian and controversialist who wrote against the Jansenists and Calvinists alike, but a humanist who published editions of early Christian writers, and an astronomer and scientist. He is one of the few theologians to have a lunar crater named after him. He is most well known, however, for kick-starting the science of chronology: the critical comparison of ancient records and other information to produce a reliable timeline of history. It was Petavius who first invented the BC system of counting for the years before Christ.

There were many attempts to use critical, scientific methods to construct a reliable chronology of world history. The most famous today is the *Annals of the Old Testament*, written by James Ussher, the Anglican Archbishop of Ireland, and published in 1650. It is strange to think that this book, which has been ridiculed as a hopelessly outdated product of biblical reactionism, should have appeared in the year that Descartes, architect of modern scientific rationalism, died. The reason for its

fame today is that many editions of the King James Bible
in the eighteenth century featured dates in the margin
to accompany the text, and the dates happened to be
drawn from Ussher's work; thus, it achieved widespread
acceptance beyond what the author could ever have
envisaged. It was in this book that Ussher argued that
the world was created in the year 4004 BC, on 23 October.
It is a statement that strikes us today as simplistic and
laughably naive, but to a man of Ussher's time and
presuppositions, it was an entirely reasonable one. After
all, Joseph Scaliger, an earlier scholar, had suggested a
date of 3950 BC for creation.

While it is sometimes assumed that Ussher and those
like him came to these conclusions simply by adding up
all the dates in the Bible, the endeavour was actually far
more complicated. Chronological vagueness in some parts
of the Old Testament, and variant readings in others,
mean that anyone hoping to establish the actual dates of
the events it describes faces a major headache – even
assuming that the narrative is reliable in the first place.
Ussher used a wide range of sources, made available
by humanist researchers and editors, in his work – the
aim of which was to establish a detailed and scientific
chronological record of the whole of world history up to
AD 70. For Ussher and people of his mindset, the Bible was
not the sole source of knowledge, although it was the most
important. The Bible and secular records alike testified to
a single body of knowledge. Here, then, we have a modern,
scholarly version of Aquinas's harmony of faith and
reason. While Ussher's conclusions may seem quaint
today, his methodology was a modern and scientific one,
although it proceeded from presuppositions that were very
much of the time.

But reason could play a more proactive role in the
defence of religion, and it was now, as the old verities began
to crumble, that many felt a new and pressing need for it to
do so. Apologetics – the task of presenting Christianity to
those outside it – flourished, although it was generally

*'I cannot open
my eyes without
admiring the art
which shines in
all of nature.
The least glance
is enough to
perceive the
hand which
made everything.
That men should
become used to
meditating on
abstract truths,
and to advancing
to the first
principles,
knowing the
divinity by his
idea, is a sure
road for coming
to the source of
all truth.'*

FRANÇOIS DE
SALIGNAC DE LA
MOTHE-FÉNELON,
*DEMONSTRATION OF
THE EXISTENCE OF
GOD* PART 1,
CHAPTER 1, 1712

intended to bolster the faithful rather than convert the
heathen. A host of pious writers produced books confirming
the belief, shared by most people since ancient times, that
God's existence and goodness could be proven deductively
from an examination of the natural world.

The most thorough and rigorous apologetics of the
Enlightenment was that of William Paley. Paley was a
rather jolly Yorkshireman, who delighted in surprising
those who expected him to be an otherworldly philosopher
by frequently making ribald jokes in a broad northern
accent. He possessed a first-class philosophical mind,
however, and came top of his year at Cambridge – receiving
the coveted accolade of 'Senior Wrangler', the most
fiendish disputant of his year. But he gave up a successful
academic career to become a rector, which he remained
for the rest of his life – despite the fame that his books,
published in the 1780s and 1790s, would bring him.

Paley was convinced that reason could provide a solid
support for Christianity. But by this he does not mean the
logical deductions of Descartes: he means the rigorous
application of the scientific method as exemplified by
Newton. Philosophy, for Paley as for the mainstream
British tradition since Locke, is a matter of advancing
arguments and hypotheses on the basis of what we
experience. It is an approach that proceeds on the basis
of induction – the notion that there is a basic regularity to
the world, and that by observing it we can form general
notions that, while not mathematically certain, can have
varying degrees of probability.

Paley put this principle into devastating effect with
his masterly *Natural Theology*, published to great acclaim
in 1802, shortly before his death. It is considered the
most powerful statement ever made of what is known
as the 'teleological argument' for the existence of God.
'Teleology' means purpose, and Paley argues that a
dispassionate examination of the world shows that many
natural objects appear designed for a purpose – and this in
turn suggests a designer. The argument had been made

countless times before, but Paley's originality lay partly in the fact that he provided a cogent defence of its underlying assumption – the supposition that an apparently designed object must have been created by an intelligent designer. This he did on the very first page

The watch on the heath

In crossing a heath, suppose I pitched my foot against a stone, and were asked how the stone came to be there: I might possibly answer, that, for anything I knew to the contrary, it had lain there for ever; nor would it perhaps be very easy to show the absurdity of this answer. But suppose I had found a watch upon the ground, and it should be inquired how the watch happened to be in that place; I should hardly think of the answer which I had before given – that, for anything I knew, the watch might have always been there. Yet why should not this answer serve for the watch as well as for the stone? Why is it not as admissible in the second case, as in the first? For this reason, and for no other, viz. that, when we come to inspect the watch, we perceive… that its several parts are framed and put together for a purpose, e.g. – that they are so formed and adjusted as to point out the hour of the day… The inference we think is inevitable, that the watch must have had a maker: that there must have existed, at some time, and at some place or other, an artificer or artificers who formed it for the purpose which we find it actually to answer: who comprehended its instruction, and designed its use.

WILLIAM PALEY, *NATURAL THEOLOGY* CHAPTER 1

Archdeacon William Paley. Engraving by R. Cooper from *The New Testament in Pictures*, published by The Religious Tract Society, London.

'Did blind chance know that there was light and what was its refraction, and fit the eyes of all creatures after the most curious manner to make use of it? These and other suchlike considerations, always have, and always will prevail with mankind, to believe that there is a Being who made all things, who has all things in his power, and who is therefore to be feared.'

ISAAC NEWTON,
*A SHORT SCHEME OF
THE TRUE RELIGION*

of the book, with the famous analogy of a watch lying on a heath. An examination of the watch shows that it is designed to tell the time, and this shows that there must have been a watchmaker who designed it for this purpose. Similarly, the fact that an eye is apparently designed to see, or a fish to swim, or the blood vessels to allow circulation, shows that they have been designed to perform these functions.

The ideal of men like William Paley was not to replace faith with reason. On the contrary, it was to bolster and reinforce faith. If Locke claimed that reason must decide whether or not a divine revelation has really happened, Paley devoted considerable energy to showing that it had. He believed that his scientific approach to Christianity led not to arid rationalism but to a living, deeply spiritual awareness of God:

I shall not, I believe, be contradicted when I say, that, if one train of thinking be more desirable than another, it is that which regards the phenomena of nature with a constant reference to a supreme intelligent Author. To have made this ruling, the habitual sentiment of our minds, is to have laid the foundation of every thing which is religious. The world thenceforth becomes a temple, and life itself one continued act of adoration.

WILLIAM PALEY, *NATURAL THEOLOGY* CHAPTER 27

Some new approaches

The staunch traditionalism of thinkers such as Paley was not the only solution available to the problem of how to relate faith to reason.

One alternative was associated with the Jansenists, the Catholic group who believed in predestination. Since these theologians tried to base their theology as closely as possible on that of Augustine, they were certainly concerned to uphold authority, and they came up with a kind of exaggeration of the medieval separation of the branches of knowledge.

This position was developed by Antoine Arnauld, the most prominent Jansenist theologian. He was, on the whole, quite an enthusiastic Cartesian, as well as a supporter of modern scientists such as Copernicus and Galileo, and he believed that in matters of philosophy and science reason should be the sole authority. But he did not think that this applied to the theological sphere, and indeed drew a clear distinction between them. When he was writing to Descartes in the 1640s, he would consciously deal with some issues 'as' a philosopher, and with others 'as' a theologian. There are some matters that reason is simply not competent to deal with, and these are things that must be accepted on the authority of the church. That's not to say that reason is simply irrelevant to religious matters – on the contrary, Arnauld thought that many religious disputes are actually about the sphere of nature rather than the sphere of faith, and should be settled by reason, not external authority.

So instead of the medieval belief in a single body of knowledge that could be accessed in two ways – faith and reason – Arnauld suggested two distinct realms of knowledge. This position was dangerous, because it meant that there was a sphere of knowledge that traditional authority had no business addressing. He accordingly got into trouble in 1656, when he refused to accept a papal encyclical concerning the doctrines of Jansen. The pope declared that certain statements were found in the works of Jansen, and that they were heretical. Arnauld agreed that the statements in question were heretical, and he accepted the authority of the pope to make such a ruling. But he denied that the pope could rule that these statements were found in the works of Jansen: surely that is a question that should be settled by the rational investigation of the books themselves, not by issuing a papal decree that we are obliged to believe without studying the evidence. And indeed, Arnauld denied that the heretical statements were to be found in Jansen's works at all.

'Were there no example in the world, of contrivance, except that of the eye, it would be alone sufficient to support the conclusion which we draw from it, as to the necessity of an intelligent Creator.'

WILLIAM PALEY,
NATURAL THEOLOGY
CHAPTER 6

For this, Arnauld was expelled from his post at the Sorbonne in Paris. Pope Alexander VII declared that the Catholic Church did indeed have the ability to make a factual pronouncement, such as whether an author had said certain things, as well as a theological pronouncement, such as whether those things are true.

To those of a more conservative religious nature, such as Alexander VII, Arnauld's approach was setting up reason as a rival to revelation and the traditional authority which embodied it. It was becoming clear that a dividing line was being drawn between the two approaches – the reliance on revelation and the reliance on reason – and Arnauld's attempt to defend the authority of reason in some spheres while acknowledging revelation in others would almost inevitably give way to a more radical sort of approach, that anticipated by Descartes, where *everything* falls within the sphere of reason alone.

One group of thinkers who started things heading down this track – the track that Alexander VII feared so much – was the Cambridge Platonists. We might be inclined to think of 'reason' and 'faith' not simply as different notions, but as opposites: 'reason' is dry and clinical, while 'faith' is irrational and emotional. But for the Cambridge Platonists nothing could be further from the truth: for them, faith and reason are the same thing.

The Cambridge Platonists were a group of academics at Cambridge University during the mid to late seventeenth century, who tried to revive Platonism, rather as the Italian philosophers of the Renaissance had done. But their philosophy was not simply that of Plato: it was more like Neoplatonism, with an overriding spiritual emphasis.

The founder of the group was Benjamin Whichcote, who argued forcefully for a completely rational kind of religion. There was no place in his scheme for taking things 'on faith': if a claim could not be demonstrated by reason alone, he wasn't interested in it. That goes for the ethical sphere as well as the religious one, and Whichcote believed that moral claims could, in theory, be proved

'I oppose not rational to spiritual – for spiritual is most rational.'

BENJAMIN
WHICHCOTE, *MORAL
AND RELIGIOUS
APHORISMS*

with as much certainty as mathematical ones.

This sounds terribly dry, but the essential belief of the Cambridge Platonists was that the application of reason and the exercise of faith were the same thing. John Smith, a student of Whichcote's, argued that God and the human soul share a close affinity: although God's reason is greater than our own, it is fundamentally the same kind of thing. This means that we can come closer to God by searching deep within our own souls, and the way to do this is through reason. It is in reasoning that we come closest to the divine life. In setting out this religious vision, Smith was consciously influenced by Origen, the Christian theologian of the third century who, a Platonist himself, was the first Christian to sketch out this vision of finding God through reason. In appealing to Origen, a notorious free-thinker, rather than the later and more doctrinaire Augustine, the authority for over a millennium, the Cambridge Platonists were deliberately championing a more open, inquisitive kind of Christianity, rather than the established orthodoxies with which they had grown up.

Rationalism

This way of thinking would lead to quite radical new developments, associated in particular with continental philosophy. In the last chapter we encountered the elaborate metaphysics of Leibniz, a rigorous account of his view of reality, as demonstrated by the careful application of logic. In fact, Leibniz believed that absolutely everything could be demonstrated by consideration of two great logical principles: the Principle of Non-Contradiction (a statement cannot be both true and false at the same time), and the Principle of Sufficient Reason (nothing happens without there being a reason for it).

A bold claim, undoubtedly; and all the bolder given that Leibniz held this to be true of religion just as much as everything else. It is a position which immediately strikes anyone who reads any of his writings from start to finish.

A gambling man

Born in Clermont-Ferrand in 1623, Blaise Pascal was something of a child prodigy. His father had strange views on education, and not only taught Blaise himself but held the commendable view that children should not have to learn maths. This simply intrigued Blaise, who taught himself the subject, supposedly discovering many of Euclid's theorems by the age of 12. He captured public interest at the age of 19, when he constructed a working mechanical calculator – anticipating Leibniz's by 30 years. He was also a major scientist – he proved the existence of the vacuum, a major problem for Cartesian science, which declared such a thing impossible.

A seventeenth-century PC – Blaise Pascal with one of his mechanical computers. Illustration from *Machines approuvées par l'Academie Royale des Sciences*, 1735.

Descartes, who met the young scientist in 1647, observed unkindly that the only vacuum he knew of was between Pascal's ears.

In 1655, Pascal was caught in a thunderstorm and had an intense religious experience. He wrote a short response to this, called his 'Memorial' – a document known only because, after his death, it was found sewed into his clothes. And he vowed to abandon the high life he had lived in Paris, including his love of gambling, and devote his life to the defence of religion, especially Jansenism. He planned a major work of apologetics, but he died, after a long and painful illness, in 1662, at the age of 39. His notes were later published as his *Thoughts*, one of the most intriguing religious works of the century.

Pascal hated the rational philosophy of Descartes, above all the way that Descartes coolly 'proved' God's existence as one might prove a mathematical theorem. Pascal believed passionately that God was not a 'thing' to discuss but a reality to experience. We can make sense of the world only by taking a leap of faith and seizing God for ourselves.

Pascal believed that this act of faith could be in accordance with reason, and illustrated it as a wager. God might exist or he might not. But the potential benefits of having faith in him are much greater than those of not doing so. Therefore, it makes sense to have faith in him – if you are wrong, you will not lose anything, and if you are right, you will gain so much. It's a wager that you can't lose.

Philosophers have criticized Pascal for not taking into account the role of probability when placing a bet. His wager works only if God's existence is fairly probable anyway. If we think it is not, then it would not be rational to believe in him 'just in case' he does exist. It would be like believing in Father Christmas in the hope of getting a present. Naturally, this is just the kind of logic that Pascal hated. The basic approach to faith developed by this iconoclastic and rather tragic figure has proved enormously popular. It offers a way of thinking of faith and reason quite different from more mainstream approaches being developed during his lifetime and in the following century.

*'Now by this
principle alone,
to wit, that there
must be a
sufficient reason
why things are
thus rather than
otherwise,
I prove the
existence of the
Divinity, and all
the rest of
metaphysics and
natural theology.'*

GOTTFRIED LEIBNIZ,
*SECOND PAPER TO
CLARKE*

Leibniz's philosophy is explained in a number of relatively short essays, most of which make for rather bizarre reading, since they begin as logical dissertations on the nature of truth and end up talking about the kingdom of God and the rule of love. Yet for Leibniz these are not really different subjects at all. He entirely rejects Arnauld's careful distinction between philosophical matters and theological ones – for him, everything is within the sphere of logic.

Despite his concern for bolstering religion with his philosophy, Leibniz did not lead a very religious lifestyle. He never went to church, and is said to have refused the last rites on his deathbed. Some people called him 'Lövenix', or 'believe nothing'. He retorted that the nickname was quite accurate, as he didn't *believe* anything – he *knew*.

Leibniz's position was set out more systematically by Christian Wolff, the most important German philosopher of the eighteenth century between Leibniz and Kant. Indeed, Wolff could claim in a sense to be the first truly German philosopher: he was the first to write extensively in German (following a few rather lacklustre attempts by Leibniz), and as a result his books were widely read and appreciated.

Wolff, who was deeply influenced by Leibniz, differed from him in being a great systematizer, and he divided human knowledge into three categories: mathematics, history and philosophy. By 'philosophy' he meant all the sciences as well as both philosophy and theology, and he argued that the aim of them all was certainty. Just as a mathematician aims to prove that his theorems must be true, and follow logically from the axioms of mathematics, so too the philosopher aims to prove that his theories follow logically from the Principles of Non-Contradiction and Sufficient Reason. Wolff was a little more modest than Leibniz, in that he felt there were some things that had not been proved in this way; and for those problems the philosopher must provide the most probable

*'The human
mind has an
adequate
knowledge of the
eternal and
infinite essence
of God.'*

BARUCH DE SPINOZA,
ETHICS II, PROP. 47

Christian Wolff,
in a beautiful
but very untidy
library. Copper
engraving, 1755,
by Johann Martin
Bernigeroth
(1713–67).

explanation. But this does not mean that there are some
areas where certainty is impossible – it is just that
philosophers haven't solved them yet. One day, Wolff
believed, they will.

This way of thinking was by no means confined to
rationalist German philosophers. On the contrary, it could
be found in a writer as different from Wolff as William
Law, the English moralist and spiritual theologian. In
1732, Law published *The Case for Reason*, in which he
argued that reason is the final arbiter of religion.
Revelation teaches us nothing that reason cannot, and
we are obliged to believe nothing that reason does not
confirm. In America, meanwhile, a Harvard graduate
named Jonathan Mayhew was repeating the same notion,
and using it to ridicule the notion of original sin which was
so important to the Calvinist tradition in which he had
grown up. This kind of rationalism, in other words, was

methods, and a very serious charge. For example, in 1670 the Reformed University of Saumur – itself notorious as a hotbed of heterodoxy – published a book entitled *The Reunion of Christianity*. It had been written anonymously by a Saumur minister named Isaac d'Huisseau, who argued that the different Christian denominations should set aside their differences and come together on the basis of the certainties set out in the Bible. His approach was similar to that of Descartes, aiming to divest himself of any uncertain notions and hold fast to what can be rationally proved. For this, d'Huisseau was condemned and dismissed by his own university – not just for his desire to overcome barriers within Christendom, which his colleagues regarded as selling out to the Catholics, but for the rationalist way in which he did so. He was branded a 'Socinian', although his theology had little in common with that of Socinus.

The reactions of people such as Frederick Wilhelm, Stillingfleet and the Reformed theologians of Saumur may seem excessively hidebound to us today, but in many ways they were quite right to be so alarmed. Paradoxically, by seeking to set the principles of Christianity on a sure and reasonable basis, apologists like Wolff and Locke were unintentionally undermining the whole edifice. All was well if you agreed with Locke that reason must judge revelation, and that revelation was up to the scrutiny; but what if after applying his method you found that revelation was not all it was cracked up to be? And if, like Wolff, you constructed a Christian philosophy on the basis of rational arguments, what happened if you found that those arguments weren't as good as you thought?

Scepticism

Scepticism means simply the opposite of certainty: it is the adoption of a doubting attitude, such as that exemplified by Descartes in his *Meditations*. It had been around for an extremely long time, and had been a powerful element of Greek philosophy. Socrates, the greatest hero of ancient philosophy, had famously claimed to know only that he knew nothing, and other philosophers tried to take this position to extreme lengths, to the extent of declaring not even to know that much.

The godfather of Enlightenment scepticism was Michel de Montaigne, a French aristocrat who lived during the sixteenth century and whose *Essays* were a series of loosely linked meditations upon human nature. Montaigne concluded that human beings were feeble creatures, whose boasts to knowledge and power ultimately came to nothing. His ideas were expanded on by his cousin, Francisco

Sixteenth-century portrait thought to be of Michel de Montaigne by the French School. Musée Conde, Chantilly, France.

Sanches, a Portuguese philosopher whose *That Nothing Is Known* was published in 1581, and who argued that, in the face of uncertainty about all matters, we must use careful scientific methods to make the most of what we can know.

Ideas like this became extremely popular in the early seventeenth century, and were used to attack the new science and philosophy just as much as they were used to demolish the old scholastic philosophy. We saw in the previous chapter how they were employed constructively by Descartes in his *Meditations*, on the principle that any ideas that could survive a sceptical battering must be certain after all.

But where Descartes hoped to turn the 'method of doubt' into a tool for discovering metaphysical certainty, others saw in it a powerful weapon of social and ideological criticism. The way was led by Pierre Bayle, whose *Historical and Critical Dictionary* of 1696 was a masterpiece of enlightened scepticism. In his brilliant and entertaining footnotes, Bayle undermined virtually every doctrine he was supposedly describing, by showing how they all led to paradoxes and irrationality. Every theory and claim to certainty, for Bayle, turns out to be arrant nonsense – none more so than the traditional claims of religion.

Bayle declared his adherence to the Reformed Church to the end of his life, but he believed that the doctrinal rigidity which he saw in that church, as in all the others, was a delusion. In his eyes, a religion can be grasped only by faith, just like all philosophy and science, because faith is all that we have. And while this may sound very pious, it does mean that Christians would never be able to refute the arguments of the atheists. Religious faith, in other words, would always be irrational. Moreover, the old distinctions between the different Christian denominations, and indeed between orthodoxy and heresy, break down. If we cannot know anything, how can one believer criticize another?

Little wonder, then, that Bayle's *Dictionary* became so popular among his successors such as Voltaire and the *philosophes*, and that others condemned his ideas as inimical to religion. It was with enlightened scepticism, above all else, that Voltaire would 'crush infamy' in the form of oppressive, superstitious religion. Yet scepticism was such a powerful tool that it would eventually prove too potent even for the *philosophes*: as we shall see in Chapter 9, in the hands of men such as David Hume, it would undermine the whole Enlightenment project itself.

**Thomas Hobbes
by the circle of
Isaac Fuller
(1606–72).**

'Among the
inferior
professors of
medical
knowledge, is a
race of wretches,
whose lives are
only varied by
varieties of
cruelty; whose
favourite
amusement is to
nail dogs to
tables and open
them alive.'

SAMUEL JOHNSON,
THE RAMBLER 17

system, Descartes asserted that the only point of contact
between the mental and material realms was human
nature. In other words, only humans have souls. Other
animals are merely complex machines, whose mechanisms
Descartes sought to unravel in his dissections. Cartesian
scientists therefore reasoned that they neither possess
rights nor feel pain; and the experiments that they
performed on animals with this attitude are the reason
why Descartes is a bogeyman to the animal rights
movement to this day.

And yet this new way of thinking would become
utterly ingrained in the western mind. The distinction
between the active subject and the passive object of study
is intrinsic to modern science. It is the ideology underlying
the science of Newton, surveying the world before him

with an impassive eye. Indeed, it is one of the paradoxes of modernity that this ideology of the scientist as observer and world as object of study would, as science advanced, eventually show that the scientists were actually just as much a part of the natural world as anything they studied, and had indeed been produced by the same processes. Darwin would overturn many of the assumptions of Descartes, but his theories could not have been developed without him.

Mechanism and mathematics

At the same time, Descartes' mechanism would also be enormously influential. Descartes was certainly not the only person at the time to argue that the physical world could be understood in purely physical terms, although he was perhaps the most famous: also important was his contemporary Thomas Hobbes in England, who went so far as to assert that the mind itself was nothing other than part of the mechanistic, physical universe. Others latched onto the same idea: we have already seen the controversy that Locke got into for suggesting that the mind *could* be material, and it was not long before the atheist Julien Offroy de La Mettrie was arguing in his *Man the Machine* that the mind was part of the same machine as the physical world. His fellow Frenchman Claude Adrien Helvetius was perhaps the most prominent exponent of this notorious view. In England, meanwhile, iconoclasts such as Henry Dodwell and the deist Anthony Collins were saying the same thing.

But the notion that physical phenomena could be explained solely in terms of material causes led to a new rigour in science, one that expressed itself most clearly in the rise of measurement as a scientific tool. Descartes himself was an important mathematician, and he recognized that if the world could be described solely in terms of extension and motion then it could be described mathematically. To put it slightly differently, what the scholastics had explained in terms of *qualities*, Descartes believed could be explained in terms of *quantities*. new emphasis on measurability was gathering mo[...] in the scientific world. Galileo, for example, who s[...] some time as a professor of mathematics at Padua[...] recognized that rigorous observation involved measurement, and indeed was as enthusiastic as Descartes about the importance of mathematics i[...] science.

The epitome of this mathematical, mechanist[...] approach to the world was the work of Pierre-Simon Laplace. Born in Normandy in 1749, Laplace originally studied theology with a view to entering the Catholic Church; but he gave that up when he discovered a greater talent for maths. After studying under d'Alembert, Diderot's collaborator on the *Encyclopedia*, Laplace set about producing a dizzying stream of scientific and mathematical papers which demonstrated, at least in his own eyes, his position as one of the most brilliant men of his age. Perhaps his most famous work was his *Treatise on Celestial Mechanics* of 1799, in which he presented a post-Newtonian account of the solar system and laws which governed it, all written in the language of mathematics.

Laplace was a major figure in French society, holding positions of authority both during the period following the Revolution and under the Bourbons. There is a famous story of his meeting the emperor Napoleon and presenting him with a complete edition of his voluminous works. Napoleon is supposed to have asked him what place God had in his system. The scientist replied: 'Sire, I have no need of that hypothesis.'

In fact, Laplace never said these words. It seems that what actually happened is that Napoleon looked at the weighty tomes with

'Philosophy is written in that great book which continually lies open before us. I mean the universe. But it is not possible to understand this book without learning to understand its language, and knowing the letters in which it is written. It is written in the language of mathematics, and the letters are triangles, circles and other geometric figures.'

GALILEO GALILEI,
THE ASSAYER, 1623

which he had been presented and vowed to read them at
the first spare moment he had; he then invited Laplace
to dinner the following night, since he had nothing else
planned! However, the exchange about God, although
apocryphal, illustrates perfectly what had happened over
the preceding two centuries. Where God and the world
had once been inextricably entwined, so that the world
made no sense without reference to God and was a symbol
of his relationship to humanity, and where any event could

The giant galactic
nebula NGC 3603
seen through
NASA's Hubble
Space telescope.

*'The motions
which the
planets now
have could not
spring from any
natural cause
alone, but were
impressed by an
intelligent
Agent.'*

ISAAC NEWTON,
LETTER TO BENTLEY,
1692

be interpreted as a manifestation of his activity and providence, the world now got on fine without God. God was simply a scientific hypothesis, to be called in as a kind of last resort when the sums didn't quite add up. A famous example of this 'God of the gaps' came in Newton's physics. Newton was adamant that, while his theories explained how the universe worked, they did not explain why the universe was the way it was: why there was a sun with planets orbiting it in the first place, for example. Moreover, Newton found that the physical laws he described didn't quite explain how the solar system could keep running indefinitely, and he had suggested that every so often God intervenes to wind up the clockwork, as it were. But by Laplace's time, even this limited role for God had been lost as the science was improved. Indeed, Laplace is remembered for his 'nebular hypothesis' of the formation of the solar system, according to which there was originally a huge nebula of gas which, under the influence of gravity, gradually coalesced into the sun and its planets. Thus, God no longer seemed to be needed even to call the solar system into being in the first place.

Secular history

If the scientists of the Enlightenment were showing how physics and astronomy got on fine without any need for the 'God hypothesis', the historians were doing the same thing in an even more subtle way. Take, for example, the work of Dionysius Petavius, the seventeenth-century theologian and chronologist. Petavius became notorious for his belief, based on a careful study of ancient Christian writings, that the early Church Fathers had not believed some of what later ages would consider to be orthodox doctrines. For example, the doctrine of the Trinity was not really known until after the Council of Nicea in 325. This claim aroused the wrath of the great Catholic theologian Jacques Bossuet, who recognized that it struck right at the heart of the Christian claim to truth. He believed passionately in the authority and infallibility of the

Catholic Church, and he believed also that the truth of its doctrines was guaranteed by their antiquity, having come direct from the teachings of the apostles and, ultimately, Christ himself. Bossuet, who may have been an inferior classical scholar to Petavius but was certainly a better theologian, saw that the notion that doctrines could have changed over the centuries – and even that the early Fathers had not believed some of them at all – was anathema to his entire system.

The dispute between Petavius and Bossuet concerned a limited issue. But it opened the door to a wider one – that of how to understand history in the first place. Can historical events – and, ultimately, the whole course of history – be understood only if we take into account the guiding hand of providence? Or is it possible to account for historical events only in terms of other historical events? The issue would come to the fore in the eighteenth century with the work of Edward Gibbon.

Gibbon had always been something of a rebel: his historical studies at Oxford had led him to embrace Roman Catholicism, and his outraged father had sent him to Switzerland to be cured by the Calvinists. Young Edward duly renounced his Catholicism, but also imbibed the heady atmosphere of the French Enlightenment, meeting with such luminaries as Voltaire. In 1776 the first volume of *The Decline and Fall of the Roman Empire* was published to enormous success. Gibbon's history was popular because of his extremely entertaining, witty style: his gift for epigram means that he is still commonly read today.

Yet the refined ladies who, as Gibbon claimed, all had his book in their bedrooms, were imbibing with the smooth words some quite revolutionary ideas. Gibbon was interested not only in *what* happened in the past, but in *why* it happened. What were the causes of the decline of the Roman empire? And what were the causes of the rise of Christianity, which occurred at the same time? Gibbon suggested that there were several factors to the latter: the devout character of the Christians, their firm belief in a

*'The theologian
may indulge the
pleasing task of
describing
Religion as she
descended from
Heaven, arrayed
in her native
purity. A more
melancholy duty
is imposed on
the historian. He
must discover
the inevitable
mixture of error
and corruption
which she
contracted in a
long residence
upon Earth,
among a weak
and degenerate
race of beings.'*

EDWARD GIBBON,
THE DECLINE AND
FALL OF THE ROMAN
EMPIRE CHAPTER 15

future reward, and their stories of miracles and virtuous lives, which were all popular. Moreover, the church provided a powerful force for social cohesion at a time when the old empire was collapsing. In other words, historical events – including the rise of Christianity – could be explained in terms of other historical events and factors. In previous times, people had assumed that Christianity had succeeded because it was true, and because its success was part of God's plan for the world.

**Edward Gibbon.
Red crayon
drawing from
*Sketchbook of
Portrait Studies*
by Thomas Patch
(1720–82).**

From this point of view, Gibbon's claims, and the assumptions which underlay them, were shocking and extremely dangerous.

Yet Gibbon went further. Not only was Christianity's rise a result of historical causes, but it was a decidedly unfortunate event. He believed that Christianity had been an enemy from within, a religion of passivity that had weakened the strength of the empire and rendered it unable to withstand the pressures from without of the barbarians. Throughout his *History*, Gibbon adopted a cheerfully sarcastic tone when dealing with religion. His expression of amazement that the philosophers and scientists of antiquity somehow didn't notice the darkness that covered the world when Christ died is typical: under a thin veil of piety, Gibbon mocked Christianity and what he regarded as its superstitious beliefs.

'When it was noon, darkness came over the whole land until three in the afternoon... Then Jesus gave a loud cry and breathed his last.'

MARK 15:33, 37

God and nature in harmony

It seems, then, that the Age of Reason saw nothing less than the wholesale demolition of the organic world view of earlier times. Yet at the same time, much of this kind of thing was, to a certain extent, the preserve of a fairly small elite. It was a fashionable, intellectual, even aristocratic way of thinking, and the older world view, seeing God in all things, was still very powerful in many quarters. We saw some of that in Chapter 4. Moreover, it was not only 'ordinary' Christians and esoteric mystics who thought in this way. There were intellectuals every bit as 'modern' as the *philosophes* who were prepared to defend it.

Two philosophers who tried, in very different ways, to reinterpret Cartesianism in holistic terms were Spinoza and Malebranche – the latter famously claiming that we see everything in God. Another was Leibniz, who felt that his philosophy of 'monads' – an infinity of immaterial substances underlying the physical world – had the virtue of showing that not only was there no great gulf between the physical and mental realms, but that the whole universe was teeming with life.

Probably the most famous Enlightenment philosopher who attempted this, however, was George Berkeley. We saw in Chapter 5 that he tried to overcome the distinction, which he inherited from Locke and, ultimately, Descartes, between mental ideas and physical objects by arguing that physical objects simply *are* mental ideas. Thus, there is no split between the mental and physical realms at all: there is only the mental realm. And more: the mental realm is

'What do I see in the whole of nature? God, God everywhere, and still only God.'

FRANÇOIS DE SALIGNAC DE LA MOTHE-FÉNELON, *DEMONSTRATION OF THE EXISTENCE OF GOD* PART 1, CHAPTER 3, 1712 also the spiritual realm. Our impressions of the 'outside' world are given to us directly by God, who in Berkeley's view acts something like the ultimate virtual reality system. Berkeley says that the regularity of the impressions God gives us is the strongest argument in favour of his existence and power, since an inferior deity would manage, at best, an inconsistent or chaotic set of impressions. Here, then, we have the notion that God's

A River Valley with a Swineherd by Martin Ryckaert c. 1610.

greatness is to be appreciated in the orderliness of the world that Newton was describing, in the mundane as much as in the miraculous. It is an intriguing precursor of the ways in which nineteenth- and twentieth-century theologians would try to overcome the objections to the notion of miracles that were put forward by Enlightenment thinkers.

Similar ideas can be found in the works of the most significant American theologian of the eighteenth century, the Calvinist Jonathan Edwards. His theology revolved around the beauty of the natural world, in which the hand of God could be perceived at every turn. In fact, for Edwards the Trinity itself is the most beautiful thing there could be, the ultimate reality that is found in this beautiful world where the colours of nature are carefully designed to please the soul, where birds sing for joy, and where spiders drift in the sky on their own silk for the sheer pleasure of it.

Edwards's philosophy, presented in a series of dry metaphysical dissertations written as a young man, was very similar to that of Berkeley, and appears to have been conceived independently of his more famous, older contemporary. Like Berkeley, he suggests that nothing exists except for God and created minds, and the world we see around us consists solely of ideas put into the latter by the former. Like Berkeley he shows this through philosophical arguments with the intention of bolstering Christianity. Edwards's vision of the world is a fundamentally holistic one, one where aesthetics and reason blend together with nature and revelation to point in unison to the Christian God.

Where Berkeley and Edwards expressed their spiritual visions within the boundaries of orthodox Christianity, one man who did nothing of the kind was the notorious and rather mysterious Emanuel Swedenbourg. Born in 1688, the son of a Swedish Lutheran bishop, Swedenbourg began his career as a promising scientist. He knew Edmund Halley and worked with John Flamsteed in London, and

God in the beauty of nature

As I was walking there, and looked up on the sky and clouds; there came into my mind, a sweet sense of the glorious majesty and grace of God, that I know not how to express. I seemed to see them both in a sweet conjunction: majesty and meekness joined together: it was a sweet and gentle, and holy majesty; and also a majestic meekness; and awful sweetness; a high, and great, and holy gentleness. After this my sense of divine things gradually increased, and became more and more lively, and had more of that inward sweetness. The appearance of everything was altered: there seemed to be, as it were, a calm, sweet cast, or appearance of divine glory, in almost everything. God's excellence, his wisdom, his purity and love, seemed to appear in everything; in the sun, moon, and stars; in the clouds, and blue sky; in the grass, flowers, trees; in the water, and all nature; which used greatly to fix my mind. I often used to sit and view the moon, for a long time; and so in the daytime, spent much time in viewing the clouds and sky, to behold the sweet glory of God in these things: in the meantime, singing forth with a low voice, my contemplations of the Creator and Redeemer.

Portrait of Jonathan Edwards, after a painting by C.W. Peale.

JONATHAN EDWARDS, *PERSONAL NARRATIVE*

Portrait of
Emanuel
Swedenbourg
by P. Kraft.

spent many years developing new technologies for the
Swedish mining industry. However, a series of strange
visions in the 1740s put paid to that. Swedenbourg
believed he had been visited by angels and the spirits
of the dead, and they had given him a glimpse of the
spiritual world that underlay the physical. Swedenbourg
wrote about what he had seen in a number of books,
the most important of which was his *Arcana Coelestia*,
published between 1749 and 1756. Although anonymous,
the book was soon known to be the work of Swedenbourg,
and he became famous as a mystic and prophet; on one
famous occasion in 1756, he described in some detail a fire

that he could apparently see raging in Stockholm, 50 miles away: subsequent reports showed that not only had there indeed been a fire but Swedenbourg's description of it was uncannily accurate. Even Immanuel Kant was interested by Swedenbourg's claims and conducted an enquiry to establish whether they were true or not: he concluded that Swedenbourg's prophecies seemed to be true, but Swedenbourg himself was no more than a dreamer.

Swedenbourg's thought revolved around the conviction that the spiritual world was far more real than the physical one. At the heart of it is God, the creator of all: yet God did not create the world as we might build a house. Rather, the world flows from God's being. God is the only true substance, and everything else depends on him for existence. The physical world which we see around us is therefore a lot less solid than it seems: indeed, it is the least real (and interesting) part of reality. Everything that happens in it is simply a reflection of an object or event in the spiritual world, such as the thoughts of angels.

Swedenbourg presented his teachings as a reformation of Christian doctrine rather than an attack on it. For example, he believed that Christ had been the whole of God, revealed in human form, rather than just one member of the Trinity; but he still spoke of the Trinity, although in a rather looser way than was exactly orthodox. He certainly got into some trouble for his ideas, but his personal popularity ensured that he escaped serious censure. Indeed, such was his influence among some that the Swedenbourgian Church survives today, still spreading its founder's message about the spirit world.

Still, the thought of Swedenbourg and, to a lesser extent, people such as Malebranche or Edwards, represented a regression back to the Neoplatonic world of the Renaissance. They wanted to preserve a vision of reality as unified and ultimately spiritual, but they were flying in the face of progress. By the turn of the eighteenth century, it was becoming clear to many that

'It has been granted to me, now for several years, to be constantly and uninterruptedly in company with spirits and angels, hearing them converse with each other, and conversing with me. Hence it has been permitted me to hear and see things in another life which are astonishing, and which have never before come to the knowledge of any man.'

EMANUEL
SWEDENBOURG,
ARCANA COELESTIA
INTRODUCTION

the future lay not in a retreat from the modern paradigm of the great divide between the physical and the spiritual, but in embracing it. These were the 'deists', and their ideas represent the epitome of Enlightenment criticism of traditional Christianity.

God in Retreat

If the scientists were making less and less place for God in their systems, the theologians were doing exactly the same thing. The latter half of the Age of Reason saw the rise and brief intellectual dominance of a curious form of religion, a sort of halfway house between Christianity and atheism, that sought to base its doctrines upon reason itself. That religion was deism, and for over half a century it coexisted in an uneasy tension with orthodox Christianity.

The word 'deism' means exactly the same thing as 'theism' – belief in God. Until the seventeenth century, the two were used interchangeably. However, 'deism' then took on quite a distinct meaning, to refer to the rationalist religion which flourished in the early eighteenth century, and which first took definitive form in England.

The roots of deism

In essence, deism was what happened when people thought of religion in terms of reason instead of revelation, as Clarke, Leibniz and the rest were doing – and then decided that some parts of religion didn't really meet reason's strict criteria. They therefore dropped these parts, resulting in a rather stripped-down version of Christianity. In Europe, one influential theologian who was doing this as early as the sixteenth century was Faustus Socinus, the Italian founder of European unitarianism, the rationalist denial of the Trinity. It was not long before similar ideas were becoming current in England, flourishing in the hands of iconoclasts such as John Biddle. Indeed, in the late sixteenth century a number of people were burned at the stake in England for denying the Trinity or the divinity of Christ. Within a century, however, it was possible to say such things without any fear of execution.

The godfather of deism proper, though, was the swashbuckling Edward, Lord Herbert of Cherbury, romantic adventurer, serial lover and literary dilettante. Cherbury, the elder brother of the poet George Herbert, was born in 1583 in Shropshire. He entered an arranged marriage at the age of 16 and, as he later claimed, remained faithful to his vows for the first ten years. He later became a Knight of the Bath, and spent many years wandering Europe as a soldier of fortune and duelist; he later claimed that a significant proportion of the female aristocracy of Europe kept a copy of his portrait between their breasts! All this ended in 1619 when he was made ambassador to France, and he died in 1648 as Baron Herbert of Cherbury.

Somehow, Herbert found time to write not only poetry and historical works, but also some surprisingly

Baron Cherbury in a typically swashbuckling pose – he is resting while out hunting, no doubt composing some verses to his latest inamorata. Published in London in 1821.

penetrating philosophy, in which he attacked the nascent empiricism of Thomas Hobbes and defended an early version of the doctrine of innate ideas, which influenced both Descartes and Locke. Herbert talked about 'common notions' which he thought were shared by all sane people, and highlighted five in particular, which he thought made up religion:

1. There is a God.
2. He should be worshipped.
3. Morality is central to worship.
4. Sin must be repented of.
5. There is a life after death, involving rewards and punishments.

Herbert believed that, in primitive times, every religion had consisted of these five notions alone. Throughout history, however, each society has added its own traditions to this basis, resulting in the diverse collection of religions we see today. In his *On the Gentile Religions*, essentially the first work of comparative religion, Herbert examined each major religion to try to demonstrate the truth of his theory.

This notion that religions – and specifically Christianity – consisted of a common core of universal beliefs, together with the irrational encrustations of history, was taken up enthusiastically by a number of thinkers at the end of the seventeenth century. They combined it with the emerging idea that religion was a matter of reason rather than revelation.

We can see the transition from orthodox Christianity to deism in John Locke's *The Reasonableness of Christianity* of 1695. Locke did not share Herbert's belief in 'common notions', a concept that he attacked powerfully in the first book of his *Essay Concerning Human Understanding*. Neither did he agree with Herbert that every society believes in and worships God; on the contrary, he thought that before Christ the only people who did so were the

'Although Luther and Calvin deserve much praise for the pains they took in cleaning out our religion from sundry idolatrous pollutions of the Roman Antichrist, yet are the dregs still left behind, I mean the gross opinion touching three Persons in God. Which error not only made way for those pollutions, but lying at the bottom corrupteth almost our whole religion.'

JOHN BIDDLE,
A CONFESSION OF FAITH TOUCHING THE HOLY TRINITY, ACCORDING TO THE SCRIPTURE PREFACE

Jews and the Greek philosophers, and everyone else was in barbarous ignorance. Christ thus plays an important role as teacher of humanity, since after him the notion of the one God and our sin in the face of his goodness has spread across the globe. At the same time, Locke stresses the need for not only illumination but salvation through Christ. This, he believes, occurs when believers repent of their sins and acknowledge Christ as 'Messiah', and he devotes considerable space to demonstrating that this was the central point of the primitive gospel message. Quite what Locke understood by 'Messiah' is not very clear, but it does seem that he was, at least, reluctant to think in terms of a Trinity. He may have been sympathetic to the unitarian tendencies of people such as Newton and Clarke – although Locke was always quick to deny that there was any kind of anti-trinitarianism in his work. Here, then, we have a rather stripped down version of Christianity. It is one where there is still a need for revelation, although it does not seem to have told us much that was not already known, at least by the Greek philosophers; but it is also a kind of 'Christianity lite', playing down the old-fashioned metaphysics and traditions. This approach is sometimes known as 'Latitudinarianism' – basically the late seventeenth century's version of theological liberalism.

The English deists

Deism really hit the headlines in 1696, when John Toland published his famous *Christianity Not Mysterious*, the basic thesis of which was that there are no miracles, no revelations, and everything in Christianity which is true can be deduced rationally. Anything else is to be rejected. Thus, where Locke believed in revelation but pointed out that reason must judge whether something is actually a revelation or not, Toland simply denied the whole thing. The same goes for miracles – if other religions claim to have miracles, and we reject those claims, then what is so special about the Christian miracles to make us believe in them? And Toland possessed a battery of arguments from history to support his view. Building on the work of Dionysius Petavius, he pointed out that many Christian doctrines had evolved only gradually, and that the Trinity and the canon of scripture alike had not been delivered from on high but had been worked out by the church in its first few centuries. Moreover, much of the Bible, such as the historical sections of the Old Testament, clashes with other authorities.

Needless to say, these ideas produced an immediate storm, and Toland was inundated with 'answers' from various Anglican worthies. But others defended the same ideas. Anthony Collins, for example, attacked the notions of reward and punishment after death in his *Discourse of Free-Thinking* of 1713, and said that people would be more inclined to act morally if they were given a rationally derived system of ethics, instead of trying to scare them with lurid tales of heaven and hell. Still more notorious was Thomas Woolston, a Fellow of Sidney Sussex College, Cambridge, whose early life is somewhat obscure. While at Cambridge he appears to have spent many years locked up for insanity. After moving to London, he set about trying to became as notorious a heretic as possible, and wrote a large number of books and pamphlets, all giving his home address so that people could come and find him and, hopefully, buy more books. He finally succeeded with his *Moderator Between an Infidel and an Apostate* of 1725, which supported Collins in attacking the clergy. His *Discourses on the Miracles of Our Saviour*, the first instalment of which appeared in 1727 and which treated the Bible allegorically to suggest that the miracles had not happened but were actually prophecies of the future, convinced many that he was indeed mad and led to his imprisonment for blasphemy.

The most famous of the British deists, however, was Matthew Tindal, who, after a lifetime of reflection on these issues, published his *Christianity as Old as Creation* in 1730. This set out systematically the now-familiar claims that, although God wants humanity to live ethically, he has not

'By natural religion, I understand the belief of the existence of a God, and the sense and practice of those duties which result from the knowledge we, by our reason, have of him and his perfections... so that the religion of nature takes in every thing that is founded on the reason and nature of things.'

MATTHEW TINDAL, *CHRISTIANITY AS OLD AS CREATION* CHAPTER 2

given any revelations: rather, he has chosen to endow human beings with reason and let them work it all out for themselves. Religion is thus a matter of following a rationally derived ethic, and doctrines such as the Trinity or the Incarnation can be safely forgotten. Like Cherbury a century earlier, Tindal believed that these doctrines had appeared after the original, 'pure' version of Christianity, polluting and obscuring its message. Tindal's work became known as the 'Bible of deism', and it was through his book above all that deism flourished on the European continent.

French deism

The works of people such as Tindal helped to make deism fashionable in France, a country where similar ideas had begun to percolate through by the end of the seventeenth century. The first real French deist was Claude Gilbert, who in 1700 produced his *History of Calejava*. The book was in dialogue form, set in an imaginary country in the far north. In his dialogues, Gilbert comes out strongly in favour of pure rationalism in religion: the character who champions the role of faith is easily crushed by the others. Like Descartes, Gilbert refuses to accept as true anything that cannot be clearly demonstrated as such. In the face of such a position, the authority of the church or scripture is meaningless. The existence of God, the nature of right and wrong, the immortality of the soul – all of these things must be proved rationally, which Gilbert attempts to do.

The relative reticence of the French to embrace deism is shown by the fact that, although Gilbert's book was printed in 1700, the printer was frightened of its contents and instead of publishing it gave all the copies back to the author, who burnt all but one. About ten years later, another work appeared which made a much greater impact – but the *Difficulties with Religion, Addressed to Father Malebranche* was written anonymously, and the still unknown author is usually known simply as 'the *Militaire Philosophe*'. As the appeal to Malebranche suggests, the author is deeply influenced by Cartesianism, and seeks to believe only what can be shown to be true. 'Faith', indeed, is a 'monster' to be fought. This is a deeply individualistic enterprise, and the author not only rejects the claims and authority of the Catholic Church but bitterly attacks them. He also attacks the Christian claim to be based on a series of historical incidents, supposedly recorded in the Bible; but reason cannot prove the truth of any historical claim. The Christian religion therefore fails the basic test of acceptability at the first hurdle. And, in fact, most of what the Bible tells us is ridiculous or patently untrue. In particular, the Trinity is superstitious polytheism; the notion of divine judgment is blasphemous; the notion of miracle is unworthy of God, because if God wants something to happen he will see to it that the universe is set up to bring it about anyway; prayer is pointless; and Christian morality is unworthy of the name.

Where the English deists – as the titles of their books suggest – saw themselves as Christians, albeit reforming ones, the French deists saw themselves as opposing Christianity. There is an anger in their works that is lacking in those of their English contemporaries, the anger of people living in an avowedly Catholic state that sought to suppress free thought.

This anticlericalism found its greatest exponent in Voltaire, who, greatly influenced by people such as Tindal and his friend Bolingbroke, representatives of the English philosophy that he loved so much, set about using deist principles to attack the whole paraphernalia of Catholicism. The other *philosophes* followed suit. The *Encyclopedia* of Diderot, to which they all contributed, was a thoroughly deist work – although Diderot himself went beyond deism to out-and-out atheism.

Lessing and the future of religion

Yet deism did not have to take this negative tone. Take the playwright Gotthold Lessing, a central figure of the German Enlightenment. Born in Camenz in 1729, it was clear from an early stage that Lessing's destiny was in the

Deism in America

Deism existed as a major religious movement for only a few decades. Yet it played its role in shaping history – for most of the fathers of the United States were deists, and both the Declaration of Independence and the Constitution show its impact.

Thomas Jefferson, for example, was well-read in such authors as Bolingbroke, Hume and Voltaire, and indeed described himself as an Epicurean, after the ancient philosopher who denied the reality of any supernatural world, including the traditional gods and religious ceremonies. And indeed, Jefferson shared the deistic belief that true Christianity is about rational morality, rather than outmoded metaphysics. In 1804, while president of the United States, he found the time to publish *The Life and Morals of Jesus*, also known as the 'Jefferson Bible' since it was an edited version of the Gospels consisting of ethics and parables with all the miracles removed. In 1787, he wrote in a letter to his nephew:

Your own reason is the only oracle given you by heaven, and you are answerable not for the rightness but uprightness of the decision.

It was Jefferson who, in 1776, drafted the Declaration of Independence, together with John Adams and Benjamin Franklin. Franklin, when not flying kites in thunderstorms, was a prominent Freemason, and a friend of Thomas Paine; and in a letter written in 1790, the year of his death, expressed his admiration for the morality taught by Christ but his doubts regarding his divinity. Adams was a deist too, and was particularly opposed to the notion of church tradition and authority; he and Jefferson both rejected the doctrine of the Trinity. Indeed, Jefferson hoped that unitarianism would, within a generation, become the universal religion of the United States.

Declaration of Independence, 4th July 1776 by John Trumbull.

'Republic of Letters'. While still at school he was writing plays and poems; when one of his first tragedies was performed in 1755, it is said that the audience remained in their seats for hours, weeping uncontrollably. But despite the popularity of his works, Lessing spent most of his life in considerable poverty. He died in 1781.

Lessing has been called the first free-thinker in Germany, but if so it was a kind of free-thinking that remained avowedly religious, even if Lessing has been called both a deist and an atheist. His thinking certainly lacked the vitriol of Voltaire and the *philosophes*. But like 'the *Militaire Philosophe*' before him, Lessing could not reconcile the apparently contingent circumstances

Gotthold Ephraim
Lessing in one of
the strangest
wigs of the entire
Age of Reason.
Oil painting,
1771, by
Anton Graff
(1736–1813).

of Christianity's appearance and development with the demand that religion should be rational. He lived in a Germany that was dominated, intellectually, by the extreme rationalism of Wolff: how, then, could Christians believe doctrines such as the Trinity or the incarnation, which could not be demonstrated by reason? Indeed, what place did historical figures such as Moses or Jesus have in religion at all?

Lessing addressed these questions in his most famous play, *Nathan the Wise*, which was completed in 1779. Tindal had believed that an original, primitive kind of rational religion had degenerated through tradition into the religions we see around us today. Lessing turned the idea on its head by combining it with the faith in progress that was so central to the Enlightenment, and suggested that the different religions were actually progressing towards a purer, unencumbered kind of religion of the future. It

The judgment of the rings

*If each of you received his ring
Straight from his father's hand, let each believe
His own to be the true and genuine ring.
… Of this be sure,
He loved you all, and loved you all alike,
Since he was loath to injure two of you
That he might favour one alone; well, then,
Let each now rival his unbiased love,
His love so free from every prejudice;
Vie with each other in the generous strife
To prove the virtues of the rings you wear;
And to this end let mild humility,
Hearty forbearance, true benevolence,
And resignation to the will of God,
Come to your aid.'*

GOTTHOLD LESSING *NATHAN THE WISE* III.VII (TR. PATRICK MAXWELL)

'I do not yet know of any place in Germany where this play could be produced, but all hail to the place where it will first see the light of day!'

GOTTHOLD LESSING,
NATHAN THE WISE,
PREFACE

would be a religion of pure rationality, when people would have learned that true religion and true morality – which are the same thing – are a matter of reason, not authority. In the play, the Jewish hero Nathan embodies these ideals of serene, enlightened, ethical reason perfectly. Nathan – said to have been modelled on Lessing's friend Moses Mendelssohn – is asked by the Turkish Saladin which religion – Christianity, Judaism or Islam – is the best. Nathan replies with his famous story of a ring which makes its owner beloved by all. The ring was handed down from father to son, until a father had three sons whom he loved equally. He therefore had two identical copies of the ring made, so he could give one to each. Naturally, the sons disagreed over who had the original, and took each other to court – where the judge dismissed their case, pointing out that who had the original ring was irrelevant. What mattered was that the sons should behave in such a way as to make everyone love them, not argue about the rings. In the same way, theological and historical arguments about religion are pointless. What matters is how we behave.

Lessing's utopian belief in a future of enlightened serenity did not, of course, come to pass. In fact, deism itself was a transitory phenomenon. With hindsight, it is perhaps easy to see that it would inevitably give way to the movement for which it prepared the ground – atheism.

Atheism

When the Scottish philosopher David Hume was in Paris, he was invited to a dinner party with a number of prominent *philosophes*. He remarked that, despite the notoriety of the atheists, he had never met one; and was surprised to be told by his host, Baron d'Holbach, that of the 18 people in the room, 15 were atheists, and the other three had not yet made up their minds.

The story shows the very different attitudes to atheism in the eighteenth century. On the one hand, atheism was a shocking and scandalous thing, to such an extent that an infamous free-thinker from Britain could claim never to have met one. They must have been viewed almost as Communists were in some quarters in 1950s America. There was much confusion about what exactly atheists were: some regarded atheism as a deluded belief that there is no God, but most people thought it was more than this, a moral failing as well as an intellectual one. An 'atheist' was popularly regarded as someone who lived and tried to justify a wanton, licentious existence. The archetype of this kind of 'atheist' was John Wilmot, the second Earl of Rochester, whose remarkably rude poems celebrate an irreligious debauchery of wine and women. Rochester regularly drew upon himself the condemnation of church figures, who regarded him and others at the court as a bad example to the nation – hence the appellation of 'atheist', although rather than actively denying God's existence, Rochester was really not very bothered about religious matters. His deathbed dedication to God and renunciation of his wasted life was widely reported and welcomed.

'Fools say in their hearts, "There is no God." They are corrupt, they do abominable deeds; there is no one who does good.'

PSALM 14:1

And to many, an atheist was something even worse – what would in future centuries be called an 'anarchist' or even a 'terrorist'. He was, more probably than not, seeking the overthrow of the state, and might well be working as an agent for the Turks. 'Atheist', in other words, was a damaging label that could mean a wide variety of things, none of them good.

But to the enlightened French aristocrats, nothing could be more sensible than atheism. It was a very fashionable position to hold, and some even regarded Hume, of all people, as something of a conformist because he never 'came out' explicitly as one of their number!

In fact, atheism, if by that we mean simply the intellectual denial of the existence of God, was an extremely new concept. There had been people in ancient times who were considered 'atheists' because they rejected traditional gods or religion. They included the Epicureans and, ironically, the Christians themselves.

David Hume

Hume was born in Edinburgh in 1711 into a fairly well-to-do family. Although he originally trained as a lawyer, he was far more interested in philosophy, and indeed had completed his most important philosophical work by his mid-20s. In 1739 he published his *Treatise of Human Nature* which, as he later put it, 'fell dead-born from the press', making very little impact. Undeterred, Hume strove to make a name for himself in the 'Republic of Letters', and found more success with various literary and philosophical essays. His *Enquiry Concerning Human Understanding* of 1748 revised the ideas of his earlier *Treatise*, and met with greater success – and notoriety, for Hume's ideas appeared to undermine not only traditional religion but even the possibility of science and philosophy as well. In 1761 the Catholic Church placed his works on the Index of forbidden books, and he began to attract considerable opposition from orthodox Anglicans. Hume, however, ignored it all, and published a magisterial *History of England*, which brought him greater fame than his philosophical work. In Britain, he was alternately praised and despised: Dr Johnson once walked out of a room the moment he saw Hume enter it. There is an apocryphal story of an old woman who refused to help the philosopher out of a bog until he had recited the Lord's Prayer to her satisfaction.

Yet despite his notorious reputation, Hume enjoyed a happy life with a large number of friends: he was invariably cheerful and morally upright, a fact which amazed many. And in France, the *philosophes* lapped him up. He was great friends with Diderot and d'Alembert, as well as Montesquieu.

Hume died in 1776. Johnson, curious to know how the notorious atheist was preparing to meet his maker, sent his sidekick James Boswell to go and see him. When Boswell reported that Hume seemed as calm and happy as ever, Johnson angrily retorted that he must have been lying.

David Hume.
Pencil, chalk and
water colour
drawing by Louis
Carrogis
(1717–1806).

After Hume's funeral, a considerable crowd watched the
graveyard overnight, hoping to see the devil arrive to carry
the heretic away: unfortunately, they were disappointed.
During the service itself, a heckler had shouted, 'He was an
atheist!' 'No matter,' replied another. 'He was a good man.'

*'If we go back to
the beginning we
shall find that
ignorance and
fear created the
gods; that fancy,
enthusiasm, or
deceit adorned
or disfigured
them; that
weakness
worships them;
that credulity
preserves them,
and that custom,
respect and
tyranny support
them in order
to make the
blindness of men
serve its own
interests.'*

BARON D'HOLBACH,
*THE SYSTEM OF
NATURE*

However, the assertion that there is no God – that the material world is all that exists – had been literally unthinkable for many centuries. But it was, perhaps, the inevitable consequence of the train of thought that began with dualism and went through mechanism to deism.

Few people 'came out' as atheists in the eighteenth century, and indeed it could still be a shocking thing in the nineteenth and even the twentieth centuries. Baron d'Holbach, one of the most radical of the *philosophes*, was an exception, stating that atheism was not only true but provided a better basis for morality than religion. Today, there are differing views over exactly what some of these people believed. Were they all deists, or did some of them pretend to be deists while really preferring atheism? Perhaps more important, however, was the fact that, whatever their personal beliefs, philosophers were starting to challenge the arguments for God's existence that had been trusted for centuries. Pre-eminent among these philosophers was David Hume.

Hume did not think much of Christianity, as is clear from his essay *The Natural History of Religion*, published in 1757. In it, Hume argued that polytheism was the original religion of humanity, but it was gradually replaced by monotheism, which was intellectually superior (just about) but morally inferior. Like Voltaire, Hume mocked the rites of Roman Catholicism:

It must be allowed, that the Roman Catholics are a very learned sect; and that no one communion, but that of the church of England, can dispute their being the most learned of all the Christian churches: yet Averroes, the famous Arabian... declares, that, of all religions, the most absurd and nonsensical is that, whose votaries eat, after having created, their deity.

SECTION 12

And the Protestants were even worse. Hume quoted – with tacit approval – the words of his fellow Scot, the Catholic mystic, Freemason, and philosopher of religion, Chevalier de Ramsay:

The grosser pagans contented themselves with divinizing lust, incest and adultery; but the predestinarian doctors have divinized cruelty, wrath, fury, vengeance and all the blackest vices.
NOTE 91

More famous was Hume's sustained attack on the possibility of miracles, found in his *Enquiry Concerning Human Understanding* of 1748. Hume argues not that miracles are impossible, but that we can never be justified in believing in them. If someone tells us that a miracle has occurred, which is more likely – that the laws of nature have been supernaturally overridden, or that the person is mistaken? There can never, Hume declares, be any evidence in favour of a miracle that would override its intrinsic improbability. He famously, and sarcastically, remarks:

We may conclude, that the Christian Religion not only was at first attended with miracles, but even at this day cannot be believed by any reasonable person without one. Mere reason is insufficient to convince us of its veracity: And whoever is moved by faith to assent to it, is conscious of a continued miracle in his own person, which subverts all the principles of his understanding, and gives him a determination to believe what is most contrary to custom and experience.
ENQUIRY CONCERNING HUMAN UNDERSTANDING PARA. 101

Hume's attacks on miracles were certainly in the deistic tradition. More radical still was his *Dialogues Concerning Natural Religion*, published posthumously in 1779. By using dialogue form, Hume avoids explicitly identifying with the views of any of his characters – but even a casual reader cannot avoid the impression that the work represents a powerful assault upon the presuppositions of theism. Hume does not explicitly recommend atheism, but he does undermine the arguments for theism.

The medieval philosophers had argued that nothing can exist without a cause, and that this must apply to the universe. Therefore, the universe has a cause outside itself, which is God. But Hume points out that the general rule to which this argument appeals is based on experience: everything we see within the universe is caused, and we therefore suppose that this is a general rule for objects within the universe at large. But why should this be true of the universe itself? We have only seen one universe, so we don't know what is normal for universes. Even if it does have a cause, why should it be a good God? Perhaps this universe is just the latest in a long series of botch jobs, made by an incompetent deity.

A version of the argument which Paley would later articulate is presented: items within the universe appear to have a purpose, and this suggests that the universe as a whole has a purpose, like a great machine. But Hume points out that even if *some* objects appear to have a purpose, that does not tell us anything about the universe as a whole. Paley's analogy of a watch is no more reasonable than the analogy of a plant – and we know that plants are not created by anyone, but grow from seeds. Perhaps this universe grew from a seed left by an earlier one.

Even if we accept the traditional arguments, Hume declares, they tell us virtually nothing. Perhaps the universe did come into being via a process rather like what we think of as design – but if so, that tells us nothing about the supposed designer. In other words, Hume's basic aim is to show that the claims of people such as Leibniz and Wolff – that Christianity can be demonstrated rationally – are false. Christianity – and perhaps belief in God itself – is nothing more than superstition shored up with dodgy arguments. To put it another way, Hume believed that religion showed just how unreliable reason could be. Instead of rationally working out what to believe, and then believing it, we actually believe what appeals to us and then provide a rational justification for it. And that leads us to make unreliable assumptions, such as the supposition that similar things, or things we choose to believe are similar (a watch, a universe) must have similar causes. In fact there is no reason to suppose such a thing at all, unless one is already prejudiced to do so. It would be criticisms like this that would strike a mortal blow not only to the Enlightenment's defence of religion, but to the Enlightenment project itself.

CHAPTER 9

The Reaction

It is sometimes easy to come away with the impression that the seventeenth and eighteenth centuries were populated entirely by men in large wigs who worshipped reason and believed that humanity was on the verge of achieving an enlightened age of serene morality and liberal benevolence. In fact, of course, the Enlightenment was just one movement among many going on at the time. We have seen in the preceding chapters how the 'New Philosophy' and its ramifications were highly controversial in many quarters, and how the rational religion of many Enlightenment thinkers existed largely in their rarified social strata, touching the religion of ordinary people only tangentially, if at all. Moreover, there were voices of dissent among intellectuals even as early as the seventeenth century, in the form of people such as Blaise Pascal, and by the second half of the eighteenth century they had become considerably louder. And many of the contradictions and problems of the Enlightenment project were forced into the general consciousness by one of the most significant political events of the century.

The French Revolution

On 14 July 1789, a mob stormed the Bastille, the great prison of Paris, symbol of the power of the regime. Its fall marked the fall of Louis XVI, the weak and foolish king of France, and the beginnings of a new form of government. Inspired by the ideals of the Enlightenment, and above all by the example of America, the new National Assembly of France adopted as its basic principles the 'declaration of the rights of man and the citizen' on 26 August, which declared as its first principle that 'men are born and remain free and equal in rights'.

The French Revolution was one of the most shattering events of the eighteenth century. It had, perhaps, been a long time coming. The court of the Sun King had not come cheap. In fact, French society was divided into three groups – the aristocrats, the clergy and everyone else – and only the third group paid taxes. Then there was the system of absolute monarchy, which worked well when the monarch was a strong man like Louis XIV. Unfortunately, Louis XVI was a terrible king, badly advised, subject to the vacillations of his wife, Marie Antoinette, and scared of the aristocrats. France's economy plunged into free-fall, and the only way the king knew to stave off disaster was to borrow money and tax the working classes still further – never daring to tax the aristocrats or the church. Little wonder, in the end, that the peasants and the bourgeoisie – the middle classes, who dreamt of a system of free trade unencumbered by prohibitive taxation – finally decided they had had enough.

The constitutional monarchy that the revolutionaries of 1789 established didn't work either, however. A combination of factors, not least war with Austria, led to the end of the National Assembly in 1792, and its replacement by the much more radical National Convention. The king was stripped of what powers remained to him, locked in a tower, and replaced with a republic. But the republic quickly became as great a despot as the king it had replaced, and whom it soon executed. A tribunal was established to weed out anti-revolutionary elements, and during the period known as the Terror, over 15,000 people were executed. No one with the slightest connection to the old regime was safe. Even Maximilien Robespierre, the head of the Committee of Public Safety and, essentially, dictator of France, found a date with the guillotine in July 1794 after his excesses scared the more marginal elements of the government. It was looking as if the republican ideals of the Enlightenment, of liberty, equality and fraternity, were either unworkable, or were no better than the authoritarian absolutism they had intended to replace.

> *'The intolerant spirit of Church persecutions had transferred itself into politics; the tribunal styled revolutionary, supplied the place of an inquisition; and the guillotine and the stake outdid the fire and fagot of the Church. I saw many of my most intimate friends destroyed, others daily carried to prison, and I had reason to believe... that the same danger was approaching myself.'*
>
> THOMAS PAINE,
> *THE AGE OF REASON*
> II PREFACE

The storming of the Bastille, 14 July 1789. Contemporary painting in the Chateau de Versailles, Musée Historique.

*'Terror is
nothing other
than justice,
prompt, severe,
inflexible; it is
therefore an
emanation of
virtue; it is not
so much a
special principle
as it is a
consequence of
the general
principle of
democracy
applied to our
country's most
urgent needs.'*

MAXIMILIEN
ROBESPIERRE,
*JUSTIFICATION OF
THE USE OF TERROR,*
1794

At the same time, the government sought to create a new society based upon Enlightenment reason. Famously, instead of the old systems of weights and measures that different countries had used since time immemorial, they decided to create a new one that was based on multiples of ten and could be used as an international standard. The currency was decimalized, as was the calendar – each day had ten hours of 100 minutes each, there were ten days in the week, and ten months to the year. Some of the country's leading scientists were given the task of devising the new weights and measures, which would be based where possible on natural quantities. The metre, for example, would be a ten millionth of the distance from the North Pole to the Equator, measured through Paris.

A major part of this revolution in society was the effort to 'de-Christianize' France. This was nothing less than an attempt to reverse completely the union of state and religion that had been epitomized by Louis XIV. According to Robespierre and his associates, the Jacobins, being a good citizen was incompatible with Christianity, a superstitious tool of oppression of the old regime. The result was the greatest state persecution of Christianity in Europe since the Roman empire. Catholic priests were forced to resign and marry, on pain of imprisonment or even death. All churches were closed and turned to other uses. The old dating system, which counted back to Christ's birth, was dropped in favour of a new calendar which counted the years from the establishment of the French republic.

In the place of Christianity, the Jacobins tried to convert the country to the worship of Reason. Many churches and cathedrals were turned into 'Temples of Reason', where celebrations were held which deliberately parodied Christian rites. It was, in effect, the first – and very probably the last – time that deism was made a state religion.

And yet the efforts of the Jacobins came, ultimately, to nothing. For one thing, with the death of Robespierre in 1794, a rather more moderate party came to power, and although public services continued to be proscribed, freedom of religion was permitted in private. Despite continued attempts to promote deism, the people showed little interest, and quickly reverted to the churches they had belonged to before the Revolution. It seemed that the revolutionaries had made a major miscalculation: they had thought that Christianity was something that the old regime had imposed on the people, and that removing the clergy would free them from it. Their failure showed that there was far more to Christian society than priests, and it was very deeply embedded in the people themselves. Christianity was not simply a philosophy or set of beliefs – it was an integral part of daily life for millions. They didn't want to be deists, atheists or anything of the kind. The religion of reason had no attraction for ordinary people.

If the revolutionaries had been paying attention to cultural developments in the preceding half-century, they might have realized this themselves.

The Scotsman and the Germans: the end of Enlightenment philosophy

We saw in the last chapter that the heart of David Hume's attacks on natural theology was his conviction that reason does not, in practice, tell us what to believe: on the contrary, we believe something first and then try to rationalize it. But this does not simply apply to religion. It is true of all apparently rational activities, including philosophy and science.

In his *Enquiry Concerning Human Understanding*, Hume devoted special attention to the notion of causation. Like other British empiricists, his interest is not in the thing itself but in our 'idea' of it, and he argues that it is a compound idea. When we think of event A 'causing' event B, we think of A happening first and B happening next, and we think of a kind of 'necessary connection' between them. We assume that, if A happens again, B will follow, just as it did before. But Hume points out that this notion of 'necessary connection' is a complete fiction. What

'Nature is always the same... therefore there must be one and the same way of understanding the nature of all things, that is, by means of the universal laws and rules of nature.'

BARUCH DE SPINOZA, *ETHICS* III PREFACE

happens is that seeing A always followed by B trains our minds to think of B whenever we see A. We then transfer this feeling of moving from the one idea to the other to the objects themselves, and assume that it means that B will always follow A. In fact, of course, while it may be the case that B always does follow A, we can have no rational guarantee of the fact. Just think about, say, a footballer kicking a ball: you can see the footballer's leg moving, and you see the ball moving, but do you see any 'causation' other than that? Do you see any 'force' being transmitted? No matter how many times you run the replay, you will only see the motion itself, and the same would be true if you had a microscope, an X-ray machine, or anything else. We can never observe the things that philosophers and scientists tell us about, such as forces and causative relations, and Hume concludes that we not entitled to assume that they exist in the real world at all.

The upshot is that induction, that procedural tool enshrined in Newton's fourth rule of enquiry and which produced such incredible results in the hands of the Enlightenment scientists, and upon which rested the arguments of Christian apologists such as William Paley, has no rational basis whatsoever. It can never be reasonable to believe that the regularities we have observed in the past will continue in the future. Yet, psychologically, it may be impossible not to believe it. Human beings simply are not rational creatures.

Hume's attack on the Enlightenment assumption that human thought is essentially rational made a huge impression on a very different philosopher: Immanuel Kant, at once the epitome and the end of Enlightenment philosophy. He was certainly the stereotype of the Enlightenment philosopher – a small and emaciated man, who lived his entire life in one town, following a lifestyle almost clockwork in its ordered rigidity, who nevertheless had the audacity to encompass the limits of space and time in his work. He was born in Königsberg in Germany (now part of Russia) in 1724, where he taught at the

'In experimental philosophy we are to look upon propositions inferred from phenomena as accurately or very nearly true... till such time as other phenomena occur, by which they may either be made more accurate, or liable to exceptions.'

ISAAC NEWTON,
PRINCIPIA BOOK III

university and, it is said, lived a life of such order that people would set their clocks by him as he passed on his walk every day.

Still, Kant was awoken from what he called his 'dogmatic slumbers' – induced by the philosophy of Wolff, at that time dominant in Germany – by the work of Hume. In particular, he was impressed by Hume's demonstration that the notion of causality comes not from observing the external world but from within ourselves. Using this as his starting point, Kant looked more closely at how the mind

'Few men think; yet all have opinions.'

GEORGE BERKELEY, *THREE DIALOGUES BETWEEN HYLAS AND PHILONOUS* II

Portrait of Immanuel Kant, 1790.

works and, in particular, where it gets its ideas from. He recognized that there were two main traditions in Enlightenment philosophy: the rationalist, exemplified by Spinoza and Wolff, which argues that all our ideas are innate; and the empiricist, exemplified by Locke and Hume, which assumes that they come only from experience. Developing arguments first advanced by Leibniz, Kant argued that the empiricists were right to suppose that we cannot know anything except by experience, but the rationalists were right to suppose that *how* we know it is innate. Hume was right to say that we cannot help interpreting the world around us in terms of cause and effect, and that we do not get this idea from the world itself. But what he did not realize was that the idea of cause and effect is, as it were, part of our inbuilt machinery for understanding the world. Just as a wearer of pink spectacles cannot help seeing the world pink, so too human beings, with a particular set of mental and physical equipment, cannot help seeing the world under a certain set of what Kant called 'categories', by which we order our perceptual world.

What this means is that the baroque metaphysics of Enlightenment thinkers such as Leibniz and Wolff was a complete waste of time. Reason can tell us things about our immediate experience, but to extend it beyond that would be like fish trying to guess what life on land would be like. Kant therefore entitled his masterpiece, published in 1781, *The Critique of Pure Reason*. He had used the methods of rational enquiry to set the limits to the abilities of reason, and he had set them in such a way that the assumptions and procedures of his predecessors were no longer valid.

In particular, Kant's arguments suggested that a lot of traditional religion no longer made any sense. If our descriptions of the world must be confined to the content of our experience, then traditional doctrines such as God and the Trinity no longer make much sense. Indeed, in line with his deistic predecessors, Kant argued that

religion was essentially about living a right life. He
thought that any religious activity which doesn't achieve
something practical is a complete waste of time. Kant was
a Lutheran from a Pietist background, and we can see that
influence on him. And although he was rector of his
university, he always managed to be 'indisposed' whenever
his presence was required at a religious ceremony.

Another German who recognized Hume's thought as a
potent weapon was a thinker of a very different character,
Johann Hamann. Hamann, who was a good friend of Kant
and indeed first introduced him to Hume's work, was a
minor literary dilettante from Königsberg, until in 1758 he
spent ten happy months living a life of extreme profligacy
in London. The financial and emotional catastrophes
this caused produced in him something of a conversion
experience: a period of intense Bible study led to his
realization that the entire Enlightenment was a dead end,
unable to appreciate the mystery of life and of divine
revelation.

Convinced not only of this but of his own genius as
well, Hamann devoted the rest of his life to launching an
impassioned attack on the Enlightenment, an attack
which drew much of its inspiration from Hume. Hamann
agreed wholeheartedly with Hume's demonstration of the
inadequacy of reason, but wondered why this had not led
the Scotsman to recognize the value of religious faith. If it
is true – as Hamann firmly believed it to be – that reason
is unable to do anything more than judge the truth of
general propositions, and that it cannot tell us anything
about the real world, then that simply shows that life is
intrinsically built upon faith. So where Hume removes
the rational support of belief, both mundane and religious,
and therefore rejects all belief as essentially fantastic,
Hamann leaves the belief intact but supports it with faith
instead of reason.

Indeed, Hamann denied the existence of 'reason' at
all, if by that we mean a kind of faculty of the human
mind, a highly polished tool which can be applied to any

problem or situation with miraculous results. That is how he believed the Enlightenment sages regarded reason, and he accused them of, essentially, creating an idol and worshipping it. There is no such thing as 'reason' – there is only our ability to think or act in a rational way. And how we think or act is determined, at least in part, by our social, cultural and political situation, which means that behaviour is rational only to varying degrees, and can never be absolutely rational. By the same token, Hamann attacked the notion of the 'idea' that had been central to so much Enlightenment philosophy from Descartes onwards. He insisted that there is no such thing as an 'idea', or an intellectual concept, of something, that exists before we express it in language – on the contrary, language shapes and partly determines our ideas. This means that our very thought-processes are determined by the language that we speak, a fact that shows beyond question that there is no faculty of 'reason' that sits aloof from our interaction with the world and with other people and pronounces judgments on what we experience. In other words, not only are the vaunted powers of reason largely useless from a practical point of view, its very existence is nothing more than an Enlightenment myth.

Instead of creating this abstract idea of 'reason' and worshipping it, Hamann suggested, we should come to a new understanding of the unity of human nature. We are not a set of different parts – 'reason', 'passion' and so on – some of which we can ignore in favour of others. God has created us as holistic entities, and we must embrace the paradoxes and dichotomies of our nature. We must celebrate the passions just as much as reason – to do anything other is, to Hamann, like castrating ourselves.

In Hamann's eyes, therefore, the bold systematizing of philosophers such as Leibniz and Wolff is just building fairy castles in the clouds. These thinkers failed to realize that 'reason' can say nothing about the world: it can deal only with abstractions, themselves the creation of the human mind, attempting to reduce the organic complexity of the real world to a series of discrete notions that can be understood. These notions, however, are just mental constructs, simple models of reality. Leibniz and Wolff wasted their time building fantastic structures out of non-existent bricks. Hamann even criticized the work of his friend Immanuel Kant on these lines. While he welcomed Kant's criticism of the overly free reign that previous thinkers had allowed to reason, he pointed out that Kant still fell into the trap of assuming that 'reason' was a thing at all, and that it functioned similarly for all people.

Hamann's ideas were developed by Johann Herder, who met him while studying at Königsberg. Herder was a Lutheran minister who, like Hamann, was tired of what he regarded as the aridity of the Enlightenment. What he most objected to was the Enlightenment's obsession with the universal. The Enlightenment thinkers had not only made 'reason' a thing, they had assumed that it is the same everywhere, indeed, that human nature is the same everywhere. That was an assumption still very dear to the heart of Kant. But the work of Enlightenment historians themselves, such as Gibbon and Hume, had shown that we are all the product of our past: that history is the story of different societies. Even assuming it makes sense to talk about 'reason' in the first place, how could, say, a German's reason work in the same way as an Englishman's, given their very different societies, histories and languages?

Like the *philosophes*, Herder believed that humanity must inevitably better itself over and against the forces of nature, but he argued that every nation must do this on its own terms and in its own way. This will mean that the different nations will inevitably conflict with each other: but we cannot judge whether this is a good or a bad thing, because the meanings of notions such as 'good' and 'bad' depend on our cultural context. Herder argued that if we want to better humanity, the first thing we must do is forget about 'humanity' at all, for that is simply a fictional abstraction. We must immerse ourselves in our own nation and culture, and seek to deepen and advance that – a process that involves taking inspiration from our own roots, and actively resisting the influence of other cultures.

This notion of the richness and uniqueness of each individual culture was, in a way, the birth of modern anthropology; for example, Herder collected and published the folk songs of different nations. Herder believed that

The noble savage

Rousseau's entry into the world was not auspicious. His mother died at his birth, which occurred in Geneva in 1712, and his unreliable father largely ignored him. As a teenager, Rousseau was apprenticed to a coppersmith, but was more interested in classical literature and ran away at the age of 16. He ended up in a Catholic school, where he embraced the Roman Church, before drifting through a variety of uninspiring jobs as tutor and musician, ending up as secretary to the French ambassador in Venice. He did compose an opera, but it was a complete failure.

Returning to Paris in the 1740s, however, Rousseau fell in with Diderot, d'Alembert and the rest of the *philosophes*, who loved his wit and his unusual views on life. These were first made known to the world in his *Discourse on the Science and Arts* of 1750, and his *Discourse on the Origin and Foundations of Human Inequality* of 1753. In these, Rousseau set out his controversial doctrine that the progress of civilization had in fact been a regression, that man in his primitive state had actually been a lot happier than he was now. Fêted by high society and adored by intellectuals, Rousseau moved between France and Switzerland, writing more sensational material, including his *On the Social Contract* and *Emile, or, Education* – the latter being the only book that ever distracted Kant to the extent that he failed to go for his daily walk, thereby making everyone in Königsberg late! However, Rousseau was not an easy man to get on with: indeed, he was neurotic and paranoid, a condition which was exacerbated as different cities and states banned him from their borders for his views. An attempt by Hume to move him to England in the 1760s came to nothing because of his inability to trust anyone; and he died something of a recluse in 1778.

the German national character involved an affinity for the soil and for nature, and a rejection of the intellectual high culture associated with France. This idea greatly influenced the *Sturm und Drang* movement in German literature, or 'storm and stress': a rejection of calm rationality and the attempt to articulate raw emotion and willpower.

Portrait of Jean-Jacques Rousseau. The cleanliness of his socks suggests that he is not getting quite as close to nature as he would have us believe.

Romanticism

This new emphasis found its greatest expression in the Romantic movement. Apart from Hamann and Herder, the godfather of Romanticism was undoubtedly Jean-Jacques Rousseau.

Like the other *philosophes*, Rousseau was a deist, and despaired of what he saw as the tendency of the different Christian churches to suppress intellectual and social freedoms and replace them with superstitious dogma. Where Rousseau broke company with the *philosophes*, however, was in his extension of this criticism to modern society in general. In his *Emile*, for example, Rousseau argued that education should be a matter of nurturing and developing the natural abilities of a child, rather than trying to fit them into an intellectual straitjacket dictated by contemporary culture. Rousseau applied the same insight to politics, and argued that every problem with modern society can be traced to the fact that the modern state tries to limit and control the natural impulses of its citizens. Rousseau argued instead that the state should be based on the will of the people, as expressed in the 'social contract' and manifested in the 'general will'.

This reflects Rousseau's insistence on the value of nature. By 'nature' he means both a historical period – the primeval time before civilization corrupted everyone – and the natural world itself, as distinct from the modern urban environment. He wrote eloquently of the solace he found in remote islands and forests, and indeed, the notion of travelling for *fun*, largely unknown before, essentially originated with him. But by 'nature' Rousseau also means something accessible to everyone, wherever they are. It means spontaneity, integrity and spiritual freedom. Rousseau calls for an end to the hegemony of 'reason' and a new sense of the whole human person, of the imagination.

It was ideas like this which would result in the Romantic movement. The Romantics hated the intellectualism of the Enlightenment and were obsessed instead with vigour, the natural world, the exceptional.

They saw beauty in disorder rather than order, a fact perhaps most clearly expressed in the changing musical fashions. Where the *philosophes* had relaxed to the cultivated tones of the harpsichord and the orderly music of Mozart, the Romantics preferred the unpredictable emotion of Beethoven, heavy on the strings.

Instead of looking forward to Lessing's age of serene rationality, the Romantics looked back to the earliest literature, untouched by the corrupting hand of civilization. As Hamann was articulating the new fetish of nationalism, the Brothers Grimm were putting together their famous collection of German folk tales, and other folklorists were doing the same in their own countries. It was in this period that William Shakespeare gained his reputation as the greatest dramatist of all time, 'rediscovered' and reinterpreted by the English as their national Bard. One of the key figures in the creation of the modern image of Shakespeare's work in eighteenth-century Britain was David Garrick, probably the most famous stage actor of all time, and a man who today would undoubtedly head Hollywood's A-List. His celebrated interpretations of characters such as Hamlet on the London stage would establish the way we still think of them, and of their author, today. Shakespeare's works were also immensely popular with the Germans, who were swept away by his unpredictability. The cult of Shakespeare, the uneducated man who managed to articulate the truths of the human soul more perfectly than the cultured aristocrats of the Enlightenment, began here.

Indeed, the concept that a proper nation ought to have some authentic folk literature was so strong that one enterprising folklorist, James Macpherson, essentially made one up for the Scottish. His 'translations' of the work of 'Ossian', the first of which appeared in 1760, were actually put together in English by none other than Macpherson himself, based on fragments of genuine Gaelic traditions that he recorded in Scotland. Despite its dubious provenance, suspected at the time but not proven until much later, *Ossian* was a huge success, becoming one of the best-selling books of the late eighteenth century. Napoleon habitually carried a copy in his pocket.

This new fetishism of the past led to a renewed interest in periods such as the Middle Ages, a time that the Renaissance and Enlightenment alike had had little time for. Sir Walter Scott published a series of phenomenally popular novels in the early nineteenth century set in a whimsical version of medieval Europe. In art, the Pre-Raphaelite movement consciously sought to go back to before the Renaissance, a programme which resulted in a large number of sentimental portrayals of an idealized Middle Ages, a time when long ringlets, enormous sleeves, and diaphanous silk gowns were apparently in fashion. By the end of the century, Victorian aristocrats were in the habit of holding mock tournaments, when they would all retire to a castle somewhere, put on suits of armour, and pretend to be knights jousting for the hand of a fair lady. In books such as *The Wood Beyond the World* or *The Well at the World's End*, William Morris transferred the age of chivalry to a landscape of his own invention, described in jarringly faux archaic language, thereby creating the modern fantasy novel.

Meanwhile, others were creating a new Romantic literature that celebrated the imagination and the wild. In England, poets such as Percy Bysshe Shelley and Lord Byron did this not only in their writings but in their lives – living fast and dying young. And the establishment of Romanticism as the new cultural status quo was sealed by the authority of Johannes Goethe, the most respected cultural figure of his time. Goethe's *Faust*, published after his death in 1832, was one of the greatest works of its age. It was by no means a wholehearted endorsement of the Romantic programme – rather, in its central questioning of the nature and purpose of humanity, the different world views of Christianity, Enlightenment and Romanticism are equally examined and set against each other.

'For my part I had rather be damned with Plato and Lord Bacon, than get to heaven with Paley and Malthus.'

PERCY BYSSHE
SHELLEY,
*PROMETHEUS
UNBOUND* PREFACE

The Enlightenment goes on

Yet it would be simplistic to suppose that the coming
of Romanticism meant an immediate end to the
Enlightenment project. On the contrary, just as
the Enlightenment itself did not sweep away the old
Renaissance and Reformation ways of thinking, but
coexisted with them, so too it continued to coexist with
the new Romantic approach to life. The development of
science continued apace in the nineteenth century, and
scientists themselves were becoming ever more specialized
and professional. The word 'scientist' itself was coined in
the early nineteenth century by William Whewell, and by
his day we can see the recognizable figure of the modern
scientist, attached to a research institute, and studying a
narrow and increasingly obscure field, replacing the old
Enlightenment ideal of the gentleman scholar or the
universal polymath. The Industrial Revolution, which the
Romantics detested so much, led to increasing urbanization
and the erosion of older, more organic, lifestyles.

Moreover, the discoveries that were made continued
the process of making God appear less and less useful
as a hypothesis. Newton had argued passionately for the
necessity of God to set up the world in the first place,
but by the early nineteenth century the study of geology
showed how much of the world's current state could be
explained in terms of its own history. Even more radically,
the fossil record was forcing scientists to find an
explanation for the apparent fact that the Earth had,
in the past, been inhabited by creatures quite different
from those found now. The theories of Charles Darwin,
published in 1859, which sought to explain this
phenomenon in terms of simple natural laws, succeeded
so elegantly that it appeared to many that science and
religion were on a collision course, never to be reconciled.

For some, the theories of Darwin provided an
excellent model not simply of how the natural world
worked, but of how society should function too. Eugenics,
the notion that human beings might be selectively

bred, was enticing to those who had inherited the
Enlightenment belief in progress and the betterment of
humanity. It was vigorously championed by progressive
thinkers such as the novelist H.G. Wells, who in his *Men
Like Gods* of 1923 described a fictional futuristic society
whose inhabitants had in this way achieved the state of
serene simplicity dreamt of by Lessing.

The criticism of progress
At the same time, of course, many felt that the new
possibilities of science were more frightening than

A romantic theologian

In 1799, it seemed to many luminaries of the Age of Reason
that religion had run its course. In the face of the advances in
science and in culture that had taken place over the preceding
century and a half, the old notions of authority, faith and even
God had been steadily eroded. Like Lessing, many felt that the
old religions would inevitably give way to a rational, universal
morality.

Many were therefore surprised to read, in this year, a highly
charged piece of rhetoric entitled *On Religion: Speeches to its
Cultured Despisers*. Its author, a 31-year-old German Lutheran
minister named Friedrich Schleiermacher, tackled the criticisms
of the Enlightenment head-on, and in so doing built a
powerful new way of doing theology that would prove
enormously influential for the following two centuries.

Schleiermacher's argument was based on the insights of
people such as Kant, Hamann and Rousseau, and it attacked
the ideas of the 'cultured despisers' at their very source. He
accepted their desire for humanity to better itself and realize
itself fully, unhampered by superstition and authoritarianism.
But if, in trying to do so, it elevates reason, and ignores the
other aspects of human life, it will never succeed. And one
of the faculties which makes us most truly human is what
Schleiermacher called 'feeling' – not simply the emotionalism
worshipped by some of his Romantic contemporaries, but self-

promising. We can see the germ of this idea in Mary Shelley's *Frankenstein*, published in 1818. As everyone knows, the novel concerns the disastrous consequences of a scientist's attempts to create life – an idea that may have been partly inspired by Johann Dippel, the Pietist theologian and real-life Baron von Frankenstein. Shelley suggests that Frankenstein's crime is not the creating of life in the first place: rather, having made his monster, he is so repelled by its appearance that he throws it out. His failure to educate the monster causes it to become a homicidal savage. Here, then, we have the notion that

consciousness, the awareness of self, and the awareness that oneself is finite and depends upon a greater reality simply to exist. In fact, Schleiermacher argued that it was impossible to better oneself, impossible to live out the Enlightenment ideal of progress, without acknowledging the central role of God.

In the decades which followed, Schleiermacher became not only the rector of Berlin University but one of the most prominent cultural figures in Germany. His ideas, developed by both himself and other theologians, would form the basis of liberal theology – one of the most important and enduring religious traditions of the nineteenth century, and one which adopted a critical, though not unsympathetic, stance to the latest cultural and intellectual developments.

Schleiermacher
by Andorff.

Eugenics in Utopia

For centuries now Utopian science has been able to discriminate among births, and nearly every Utopian alive would have ranked as an energetic creative spirit in former days. There are few dull and no really defective people in Utopia; the idle strains, the people of lethargic dispositions or weak imaginations, have mostly died out; the melancholic type has taken its dismissal and gone; spiteful and malignant characters are disappearing. The vast majority of Utopians are active, sanguine, inventive, receptive and good-tempered.

H.G. WELLS, *MEN LIKE GODS* BOOK 1, CHAPTER 5

scientific progress might fail to be matched by moral progress. Dr Frankenstein is an exemplary Enlightenment scientist, but his sense of moral responsibility is sadly lacking compared to his medical ability.

By the end of the nineteenth century, many writers were exploring the notion that scientific progress itself might be a form of moral regress. It was an idea that had such good dramatic possibilities that even progressive heirs to the Enlightenment such as H.G. Wells used it. His novel *The Invisible Man*, published in 1897, describes the consequences of a scientist's experiment to turn himself invisible. Unable to interact with normal society, the scientist becomes gradually more and more unhinged. Finally, the power which his invisibility gives him over others becomes too much to handle, and he succumbs to homicidal madness before being tracked down and killed – with difficulty – by a mob. In other words, the advance of science, the power it may confer, and the effect on traditional society that it can cause, can itself be an ethical step backwards. The pinnacle of this gloomy outlook would be Aldous Huxley's *Brave New World* of 1932, a satire on Utopian dreams of the past, presenting a vision of a future where everyone is bio-engineered and drugged into a blandly uniform happiness, but where there is no true morality or value of any kind.

To many, such scepticism was vindicated by the terrible events of much of the twentieth century. The eugenics programme of the Nazis revealed exactly what the cost of that ideal could be. The slaughter of two world wars suggested that humanity had not done much advancing since the eighteenth century, and that Lessing's serene, enlightened future was as far off as it ever was. And in the latter half of the twentieth century, people had to contend with the fact that the spirit of scientific enquiry epitomized by Newton and his modern successor, Einstein, had produced the atomic bomb. Here was a weapon so awesome that its use in anger might threaten the existence of civilization itself. If anything, it seemed that the scientific advances of the Enlightenment and the following period had produced moral regression, not progress.

Today, it has become widely acknowledged that scientific advances open up just as many terrifying prospects as they do beneficial ones. Debates over issues such as genetic engineering show how ingrained the principle has become for many people that *can* does not imply *should*.

The legacy

In the twenty-first century, we live in a world which the savants of the Age of Reason would barely recognize. Yet it is easy to see that the awesome technological advances that have marked the intervening two centuries have been a side product, as it were, of the faith in reason's ability to understand the world, and in humanity's ability to improve itself, that inspired the science of the Enlightenment. More subtle, but just as important, are the legacies of Enlightenment thought and society that still influence us today.

It is a commonplace, in an age of email and cheap air fares, that we inhabit a rapidly shrinking world – a global village where one may flirt with a stranger in Bangalore or bid in an auction in Tokyo. A century of devastating

*'If each man
wholly and
immediately
directs all his
thoughts to his
own interest…
the whole
human race
together will be
immersed in the
deepest
wretchedness.
Let us therefore
endeavour to
promote the
general
happiness of
mankind; all
mankind, in
return, will
endeavour to
promote ours,
and thus we
shall establish
our felicity on
the most solid
foundations.'*

EMMERICH VON
VATTEL, *THE LAW OF
NATIONS*,
PRELIMINARIES
PARA. 10

warfare has taught us to value the bonds of common
humanity between the nations, and to try to create bodies
such as the United Nations to enshrine and enforce
international law. These are notions and ideals which the
Enlightenment thinkers would recognize. One of their
greatest desires was to overcome the barriers they
perceived between different peoples – whether cultural,
intellectual or religious – and learn to embrace a common
humanity. Take, for example, the Swiss philosopher
Emmerich von Vattel, who in his *Law of Nations* of 1758
used the thought of Wolff as a starting point to urge an
enlightened world of nations all acting for the common
good, a kind of global federation of goodwill. History since
1758 may have conspired to show that such a world is hard
to achieve, yet it is an ideal which we can still recognize
and from which we can take inspiration.

Indeed, Vattel's notion that individuals and nations
alike are duty-bound to act not in their own interests, or in
the interests of a certain class, but in the interests of all
people, is fundamental to our modern ideals of democratic
government. The idea of a democracy would, perhaps, have
been a little advanced for most of the Enlightenment
thinkers, who were well aware of their own status as
members of society's elite. But the notions of fundamental
human rights which underlie our modern democratic ideals
were not only hammered out in the Enlightenment but
first tested then too. The absolute monarchies of the early
seventeenth century had, by the nineteenth, largely given
way to constitutional monarchies – where the monarch
rules in name only, as in Britain – or to republics, where
the people rule themselves. We live by the same model of
politics and society today.

And the Enlightenment thinkers did not just conceive
of a world in harmony and liberty: they dreamt of a world
of progress and reason. That meant education. In place of
the old static system of the Middle Ages, where everyone
had their place, ordained by God, the Enlightenment
thinkers believed that human beings should strive to

improve themselves, so that eventually everyone could belong to the intellectual elite. Exactly how this should be done was a moot point. In *Emile*, for example, Rousseau argued that children should be educated at home, to avoid the corrupting influence of French society; but others felt that it was more productive to reform national education systems. Thomas Jefferson, for example, sought to provide three years of free schooling to all white children in Virginia – which was at least a step in the right direction.

Perhaps the greatest figure in this endeavour was August Francke, a Pietist theologian who was also Professor of Oriental Studies at the University of Halle at the turn of the eighteenth century. Like other Pietists, Francke felt that the Reformation had yet to be completed, but he believed that it had to spread beyond the church and reform society itself. The key to this was education, and Francke made radical changes to the education system not only of his university but of his whole city. He believed that a student should advance on the basis of merit, not of wealth, and he tried to build Halle's education system around this principle, as well as his conviction that education should train the whole person, not just the mind. The ideal, dear to many today, that free education is a right, would have been unheard of before Francke's time; and it was the efforts of him and others like him that laid the foundation for the more open and merit-based education systems of today.

And what of the Enlightenment's contribution to religion? At first glance it is less easy to be positive about that, at least if one is religious. After all, it was the Enlightenment that launched a tremendous assault on the accepted orthodoxies of the past; it was the Enlightenment that gave us biblical criticism, which has swept away many cherished beliefs about the provenance and meaning of the scriptures; it was the Enlightenment thinkers who sought to discard old doctrines such as the Trinity; it was the Enlightenment that first set science and

'Of all the men we meet with, nine parts of ten are what they are, good or evil, useful or not, by their education.'

JOHN LOCKE,
SOME THOUGHTS CONCERNING EDUCATION PART 1

religion against each other; and it was the Enlightenment that gave us modern atheism. Little wonder that many Christians might regard the seventeenth and eighteenth centuries as a period of darkness rather than of light, when people abandoned the truths of the gospel to follow a fake idol of their own creation, human reason.

That may be one way of viewing it; but of course the Enlightenment thinkers would not have agreed. In their eyes, they were continuing the tradition of Anselm of Canterbury, the eleventh-century theologian whose famous slogan was 'faith seeking understanding' – the ideal of trying to understand the content of faith through rational enquiry. Today, many theologians try to balance the different potential sources of doctrine – scripture, tradition, the authority of the church and reason – rather than treat a single one of these as all-important. Part of that programme is viewing each source with a critical eye on the basis of the others. To put it simplistically, that is what Luther and his colleagues did in the Reformation, when they criticized the church on the basis of scripture; and so, too, did Enlightenment figures such as Socinus, the deists, or Locke when they criticized the heritage of the Reformation on the basis of reason. Like all rebels, the Enlightenment theologians acted out important principles, and offer a valuable model, even to those who disagree with what might have been their excesses.

And in their criticism of traditional religion, the Enlightenment thinkers played a central role in the creation of our modern world. The Enlightenment was the first time, since the initial evangelization of Europe during the Roman empire and the Dark Ages, when Christianity and secular culture separated. In the Middle Ages and the Renaissance, culture *was* Christian. But the work of Bayle, Voltaire, Hume and the rest, iconoclasts though they may have been, helped to separate the two – to subject Christianity to a merciless criticism, from the viewpoint of modern, enlightened, rational culture. In so doing, they created a dialogue that could go both ways – as they found when Schleiermacher published his *Speeches*. Christianity, from now on, was to a certain extent on the defensive, and it is since the Enlightenment that the West has seen the gradual erosion of the privileged position that Christianity once held. But this meant that the religion could also go on the offensive. The fact that Christianity was no longer the sole authority meant that it could attack authority, that it could be culturally, morally or even politically subversive. That would happen later when, for example, Christians were among those who opposed the slave trade, or who fought for the underprivileged in South America, or who campaigned for the cancellation of Third World debt. And it might be said that that is a far better position for Christianity to be in – a position that harks back to the radical poverty of St Francis of Assisi, to the uncompromising witness of the martyrs of the early church, and to the message of Jesus himself.

Chronology

1625: Hugo Grotius, *On the Law of Peace and War*.

1628: William Harvey, *On the Motion of the Heart and Blood in Animals*.

1632: Galileo Galilei, *Dialogue Concerning the Two Chief World Systems*.

1637: René Descartes, *Discourse on Method*.

1640: First London stagecoach service. Cornelius Jansen, *Augustinus*.

1641: René Descartes, *Meditations on the First Philosophy*.

1642–51: English Civil War.

1644: Dionysius Petavius, *Dogmatic Theology*.

1645: Conference of the Thorn tries to unify the European churches.

1647: Johannes Hevelius publishes the first map of the moon. George Fox founds the Society of Friends.

1648: The Treaty of Westphalia ends the Thirty Years War.

1649: Execution of King Charles I of England.

1650: James Ussher, *Annals of the Old Testament*.

1651: Thomas Hobbes, *Leviathan*.

1656: Christian Huygens invents the pendulum clock.

1656–57: Blaise Pascal, *Provincial Letters*.

1659: Christian Huygens describes the landscape of Mars.

1660: Restoration of King Charles II of England. Cuckoo clock invented in Germany.

1661: King Louis XIV of France begins his personal rule. Marcello Malpighi discovers capillaries.

1662: Antione Arnauld and Pierre Nicole, *Port Royal Logic*. Royal Society of London established.

1665: Robert Hooke describes plant cells. Sir Isaac Newton discovers the differential calculus.

1666: Great Fire of London. French Royal Academy of Sciences founded. Sir Isaac Newton discovers the refraction of light.

1667: John Milton, *Paradise Lost*. Jean Baptiste Denis performs the first blood transfusion.

1668: Sir Isaac Newton invents the reflecting telescope. Antony Van Leeuwenhoek discovers red blood cells. Jacques Bossuet, *Exposition of Catholic Doctrine*.

1669: John Wagstaffe, *The Question of Witchcraft Debated*.

1670: Blaise Pascal, *Thoughts*.

1672: France invades Holland – Amsterdam is flooded to keep the French out.

1674: Nicolas Malebranche, *The Search for Truth*.

1675: Antony van Leeuwenhoek discovers protozoa. John Flamsteed founds the Greenwich Observatory. Philip Spener, *Pious Wishes*. Olaus Romer calculates the speed of light.

1677: Baruch de Spinoza, *Ethics*.

1678: Ralph Cudworth, *The True Intellectual System of the Universe*.

1681: Jacques Bossuet, *Discourse on Universal History*. The Canal du Midi opens, linking the Bay of Biscay to the Mediterranean. Russian Academy of Sciences founded.

1682: Pennsylvania founded by William Penn. Louisiana claimed in the name of Louis XIV of France. French court moved to Versailles. Sir Edmund Halley observes his comet.

1683: Siege of Vienna ends with the rout of

the Turks. Antony van Leeuwenhoek discovers bacteria.

1685: King Louis XIV revokes the Edict of Nantes.

1687: Sir Isaac Newton, *Principia*.

1688: English Glorious Revolution.

1689–97: The War of the Grand Alliance – France versus almost everyone else.

1690: John Locke, *Essay Concerning Human Understanding*. Christian Huygens proposes that light is a wave.

1692: Salem witch trials.

1694: *The Dictionary of the French Academy*.

1695: Gottfried Leibniz, *The New System of Nature*. John Locke, *The Reasonableness of Christianity*.

1696: Pierre Bayle, *Historical and Critical Dictionary*. John Toland, *Christianity Not Mysterious*.

1698: Tsar Peter the Great of Russia travels through Europe. Thomas Savery patents the first steam engine.

1699: Gottfried Arnold, *Impartial History of the Church*.

1700: Berlin Academy of Science founded.

1702–13: War of the Spanish Succession, England and Holland against France.

1703: St Petersburg founded.

1710: George Berkeley, *The Principles of Human Knowledge*. 'Militaire Philosophe', *Difficulties with Religion*.

1712: François de Salignac de La Mothe-Fénelon, *Demonstration of the Existence of God*.

1713: Christian Wolff, *German Logic*. Anthony Collins, *Discourse of Free-Thinking*.

1714: Gottfried Leibniz, *Monadology*. Gabriel Fahrenheit invents the mercury thermometer. Alexander Pope's translation of the *Iliad*.

1720: The South Sea Bubble – the first stock market crash – bankrupts thousands.

1723: King Frederick I of Prussia exiles Christian Wolff.

1726: Jonathan Swift, *Gulliver's Travels*.

1728: William Law, *A Serious Call to a Devout and Holy Life*.

1729: Stephen Gray discovers the conductivity of electricity. Johann Sebastian Bach, *St Matthew's Passion*. Johann Dippel, *True Evangelical Demonstration*.

1730: Matthew Tindal, *Christianity as Old as Creation*.

1732: William Law, *The Case for Reason*.

1733: John Kay patents the flying shuttle loom.

1734: Voltaire, *Philosophical Letters*.

1735: Rubber discovered in South America.

1736: Witchcraft no longer a capital crime in England.

1737: Carolus Linnaeus invents the binomial classification system.

1738: John Wesley experiences his evangelical conversion.

1739: David Hume, *Treatise of Human Nature*.

1739–42: War of Jenkins' Ear between Britain and Spain.

1740: Frederick the Great becomes King of Prussia and recalls Wolff.

1741: Georg Handel, *Messiah*. First suspension bridge, at Tees.

1743–48: King George's War in the Americas.

1745: Jacques Daviel performs the first cataract operation.

1746: Jonathan Edwards, *Treatise Concerning Religious Affections*.

1758: Baron Montesquieu, *The Spirit of the Laws*. Julien Offroy de La Mettrie, *Man the Machine*. David Hume, *Enquiry Concerning Human Understanding*.

1749: Henry Fielding, *Tom Jones*.

1749–56: Emanuel Swedenbourg, *Arcana Coelestia*.

1751–52: Denis Diderot and Jean d'Alembert, *Encyclopaedia*.

1752: Benjamin Franklin invents the lightning conductor. Daniel Bernouilli invents the ship's propeller.

1755: Samuel Johnson, *Dictionary of the English Language*. Lisbon earthquake.

1756–63: Seven Years War: France, Austria, Russia, and Sweden versus Prussia and Britain.

1757: David Hume, *The Natural History of Religion*.

1758: Emmerich von Vattel, *Law of Nations*.

1759: Voltaire, *Candide*.

1760: George III becomes King of England. James Cox builds a 'perpetual motion' clock that runs forever. John Merlin invents roller skates, wears them to a party, and nearly suffers serious injury.

1761: Mikhail Lomonosov discovers the atmosphere of Venus.

1762: Jean-Jacques Rousseau, *The Social Contract*. Catherine the Great becomes Tsarina of Russia.

1764: James Hargreaves invents the Spinning Jenny. Voltaire, *Philosophical Dictionary*.

1765: The Stamp Act outrages Britain's American colonies.

1767: Laurence Sterne, *Tristram Shandy*.

1768: Joseph Priestly invents carbonated water.

1769: James Watt patents his steam engine. Nicolas Cugnot builds the first steam-powered car.

1770: Baron d'Holbach, *The System of Nature*.

1774: Louis XVI becomes King of France. Johann Goethe, *The Sorrows of Werther*. Joseph Priestly discovers oxygen.

1775: Alexander Cummins patents the WC.

1776: Thomas Paine, *Common Sense*. Edward Gibbon, *Decline and Fall of the Roman Empire*. American *Declaration of Independence* written.

1777: Americans invent the torpedo.

1778: France allies with America against Britain. Catholic Relief Act decriminalizes Catholicism in Britain.

1779: Gotthold Lessing, *Nathan the Wise*. David Hume, *Dialogues Concerning Natural Religion*.

1779–81: Samuel Johnson, *Lives of the Poets*.

1781: Immanuel Kant, *Critique of Pure Reason*. William Herschel discovers Uranus.

1782: Jean-Jacques Rousseau, *Confessions*.

1783: Peace of Versailles ends American War of Independence. Montgolfier brothers launch first manned balloon.

1784–91: Johann Herder, *Ideas Toward a Philosophy of a History of Mankind*.

1785: John Jeffries makes the first air crossing of the English Channel. W.A. Mozart, *The Marriage of Figaro*. Edmund Cartwright invents the power loom.

1787: Constitution of the United States of America signed. First working telegraph demonstrated in Paris. John Fitch launches the first steam ship.

1788: Immanuel Kant, *Critique of Practical Reason*.

1789: William Blake, *Songs of Innocence*. French Revolution. Antione Lavoisier, *Elements of Chemistry*. Pierre-Simon Laplace, *Laws of the Planetary System*.

1790: Immanuel Kant, *Critique of Judgment.*

1791: Marquis de Sade, *Justine.* Thomas Paine, *The Rights of Man.*

1792: William Murdock invents gas lighting. Execution of King Louis XVI of France.

1792–95: French revolutionary wars.

1793: Thomas Paine, *The Age of Reason.*

1795: Metric system adopted in France. William Paley, *Evidences of Christianity.*

1796: Edward Jenner carries out the first vaccination against smallpox.

1798: Henry Cavendish calculates the earth's mass. Thomas Malthus, *Essay on the Principle of Population.*

1799: Humphry Davy discovers nitrous oxide, the first anaesthetic. Napoleon Bonaparte becomes First Consul of France. Pierre-Simon Laplace, *Treatise on Celestial Mechanics.* Friedrich Schleiermacher, *Speeches on Religion.*

1800: Ludwig Van Beethoven, *First Symphony.*

1802: William Paley, *Natural Theology.*

1804: Napoleon Bonaparte becomes Emperor of France.

Suggestions for Further Reading

Books about the period in general

E. Cameron (ed.), *Early Modern Europe: An Oxford History*, Oxford: Oxford University Press, 2001.

N. Hampson, *The Enlightenment*, Harmondsworth: Penguin, 1968.

G. Havens, *The Age of Ideas: From Reaction to Revolution in Eighteenth-Century France*, New York: Holt, 1955.

P. Hazard, *European Thought in the Eighteenth Century, from Montesquieu to Lessing*, London: Hollis and Carter, 1954.

M. Jacob, *The Radical Enlightenment*, London: Allen & Unwin, 1981.

D. Outram, *The Enlightenment*, Cambridge: Cambridge University Press, 1995.

J. Redwood, *Reason, Ridicule and Religion: The Age of Enlightenment in England, 1660–1750*, London: Thames and Hudson, 1976.

J. Sprink, *French Free Thought from Gassendi to Voltaire*, London: University of London Press, 1960.

J. Yolton, R. Porter, P. Rogers and B. Safford (eds), *The Blackwell Companion to the Enlightenment*, London: Blackwell, 1991.

Books about particular figures and movements

D. Adamson, *Blaise Pascal: Mathematician, Physicist and Thinker about God*, Basingstoke: Macmillan, 1995.

J. Cottingham, *Descartes*, Oxford: Blackwell, 1986.

E. Foner, *Tom Paine and Revolutionary America*, Oxford: Oxford University Press, 1976.

C. Fox, R. Porter and R. Wokler (eds), *Inventing Human Science: Eighteenth-Century Domains*, Berkeley, CA: University of California Press, 1995.

J. Gaskin, *Hume's Philosophy of Religion*, New York: Macmillan, 1978.

J. Herrick, *The Radical Rhetoric of the English Deists: The Discourse of Skepticism, 1680–1750*, Columbia, SC: University of South Carolina Press, 1997.

E. Kremer (ed.), *The great Arnauld and Some of his Philosophical Correspondents*, Toronto, London: University of Toronto Press, 1994.

D. LeMahieu, *The Mind of William Paley: A Philosopher and his Age*, Lincoln, NE: University of Nebraska Press, 1976.

J. Marshall, *John Locke: Resistance, Religion and Responsibility*, Cambridge: Cambridge University Press, 1994.

H. Martin, *Puritanism and Richard Baxter*, London: SCM Press, 1954.

F. Powicke, *The Cambridge Platonists: A Study*, Westport, CN: Greenwood Press, 1970.

J. Smith, *Jonathan Edwards*, London: Geoffrey Chapman, 1992.

K. Stein, *Philipp Jakob Spener: Pietist Patriarch*, Chicago: Covenant Press, 1986.

N. Torrey, *Voltaire and the English Deists*, Hamden, CT: Archon Books, 1967.

J. Turner, *John Wesley: The Evangelical Revival and the Rise of Methodism in England*, Peterborough: Epworth, 2002.

I. Wade, *The Intellectual Development of Voltaire*, Princeton, NJ: Princeton University Press, 1969.

A. Walker, *William Law: His Life and Thought*, London: SPCK, 1973.

R. Westfall, *Never at Rest: A Biography of Isaac Newton*, Cambridge: Cambridge University Press, 1980.

Books by some of the authors themselves

P. Bayle, *Historical and Critical Dictionary: Selections*, Indianapolis: Hackett, 1991.

G. Berkeley, *Three Dialogues Between Hylas and Philonous*, Oxford: Oxford University Press, 1998.

J. Bossuet, *Politics Drawn from the Very Words of Holy Scripture*, Cambridge: Cambridge University Press, 1990.

R. Descartes, *Philosophical Essays and Correspondence*, Indianapolis: Hackett, 2000.

D. Hume, *Dialogues Concerning Natural Religion*, London: Routledge, 1991.

W. Law, *The Works of the Reverend William Law*, Bristol: Thoemmes Press, 2000.

G.W. Leibniz, *Philosophical Writings*, London: Everyman, 1973.

J. Locke, *Essay Concerning the True Original Extent and End of Civil Government; The Second Treatise of Government; A Letter Concerning Toleration*, Mineola, NY: Dover, 2002.

W. Paley, *Natural Theology; or, Evidences of the Existence and Attributes of the Deity, Collected from the Appearances of Nature*, Farnborough: Gregg, 1970.

B. Pascal, *Pensées and other Writings*, Oxford: Oxford University Press, 1999.

B. Spinoza, *Ethics*, London: Everyman, 1993.

Voltaire, *Candide*, London: Penguin, 2001.

Index

Picture and Text Acknowledgments

Pictures

Picture research by Zooid Pictures Limited.

AKG – Images: pp. 20–21, 102, 108–109, 129, 162, 179, 191; 4, 16, 31, 96 (Erich Lessing); 174–75 (Chateau de Versailles, Musée Historique).

Bridgeman Art Library: pp. 27, 71, 88, 144; 2–3 (Verby Museum and Art Gallery, UK), 133 (Lauros/Giraudon), 138 (Burghley House Collection, Lincolnshire, UK), 167 (Scottish National Portrait Gallery, Edinburgh, Scotland).

Corbis UK Ltd: pp. 1 (NASA/Roger Ressmeyer); 8, 18–19, 32, 46, 61, 63, 91, 149, 160–61 (Bettmann); 13 (Arte & Immagini srl), 28–29 (Macduff Everton); 35, 38, 54–55, 150 (Archivo Iconografico, S.A.); 43 (Kristi J. Black), 57 (Gianni Dagli Orti), 66–67 (Francis G. Mayer), 74 (Bojan Brecelj), 116–17 (Pizzoli Alberto Sygma), 146–47 (Christie's Images), 185 (Leonard de Selva).

Hulton|Archive/Getty Images: p. 111.

Mary Evans Picture Library: pp. 52, 83 (Illman), 121 (R. Cooper), 154 (H.R. Cook after a painting by Isaac Oliver).

NASA: pp. 140–41.

Science Photo Library: pp. 65 (Dr Brian Ford), 126.

Lion Hudson

Commissioning editor: Morag Reeve

Project editor: Olwen Turchetta

Designer: Nicholas Rous

Production manager: Kylie Ord